MW01013589

Fran

Franklin Smoke

FRANKLIN
SMOKE

WOOD · FIRE · FOOD

AARON FRANKLIN
and
JORDAN MACKAY

Photographs by Wyatt McSpadden

TEN SPEED PRESS
California | New York

Contents

Preface

In 2021, Daniel Vaughn, *Texas Monthly*'s barbecue editor and a writer who continues to make a sizeable and underappreciated contribution to this country's food literature, penned a profound piece in that magazine. "After 411 joints tested," he wrote, "I can confidently report that our favorite smoked meat [brisket] is so reliably excellent in all parts of Texas that it no longer feels like an achievement. Texas brisket has peaked."

Vaughn notes that he's not complaining but rather marking this moment with appreciation, as in the past, "praiseworthy smoked brisket was the bovine equivalent of unobtainium for entire regions of Texas."

The piece was of particular meaning to people named Franklin and those associated with them because, as Vaughn wrote:

> I can tell you exactly when this path to excellence began: December 2009, when Aaron and Stacy Franklin started selling their smoked brisket in Austin. . . . Copycat joints—I won't name names because there are too many—started to pop up. Then Franklin wrote down all of his smoky secrets in *Franklin Barbecue: A Meat-Smoking Manifesto*, published in 2015. He had written an instruction manual and handed it to his competitors. When the most famous brisket cook the world has ever seen tells you exactly how to replicate his cash cow, enterprising pitmasters are going to do exactly that. Much of our current glut of superlative smoked brisket comes from barbecue joints that opened in the post-Franklin barbecue world . . . a whole lot of Texas brisket tastes like we're eating a cover song. Granted, it's a cover of the greatest barbecue tune ever written.

I quote at such length because the writing is good and perfectly explains the situation. In today's world, so rich with great barbecue, it's hard to imagine a time when truly tender, crusty brisket didn't really exist. I grew up in Austin in the 1980s and '90s and ate barbecued brisket mostly on special occasions. I don't remember ever being wowed by it.

In Aaron's decision to teach the world how to cook brisket just the way he does lies a certain contradiction: he remains somewhat competitive. Not with any single person or restaurant, but with the entire brisket-making establishment that he helped create. Aaron cares deeply—and he and Stacy work very hard—to ensure that the quality at Franklin Barbecue never dips. As he's seen other barbecue joints arise all over the state touting world-class brisket—and, as Vaughn notes, many of these pitmasters probably learned brisket technique from the book, while a few learned the craft directly from having worked at Franklin—he's taken it in stride and applauds new success stories, even as he doubles down on his restaurant's own efforts to remain top quality, which is no easy feat.

In a world where even top restaurants have trouble finding dishwashers and servers, recruiting people to work long hours tending fires in the Texas summer is even harder. Training them in the art of brisket (and other meats) is another story. Of course, Franklin Barbecue's success is not just about the quality of the brisket. All the food is good, but I maintain that the friendliness of the staff and the cheery hospitality customers receive there makes for an exceedingly satisfying experience worth repeatedly waiting in line for, which many people do. That spirit is in the restaurant's DNA and can't be taught in a book.

One thing about Texas in the era of Peak Brisket that's easy to overlook, yet can't be overstated, is that making and selling world-class brisket is never easy. Rather, it requires supreme effort, beginning with building or buying a costly, massive smoker and then devoting long, often thankless, nocturnal hours to cooking.

No matter who you are, it's a challenge to produce a great brisket once, let alone daily, and Aaron not only respects that, but applauds it. So even as sharing brisket-smoking technique has fostered new competition, Aaron recognizes the cost and effort required to produce good barbecue and create a sustainable business. For that, I know he wishes everyone the best.

Especially gratifying is that, in this digital world full of distraction and abstraction, so many people are taking up the challenge of slowing down and cooking with the elements. There are few slower "slow foods" than brisket, which we revisit in these pages. We also feature several other techniques that require the time and effort of building a fire, creating a strong coal bed, and then cooking slowly over it to get layers and layers of flavor and texture. As is Aaron's way, he's far more interested in technique than in the specific ingredients in sauces and seasonings, which he's more than happy to leave up to your own individual preferences.

Cooking anything—but especially large cuts of meat—with fire and smoke is one of the most challenging and gratifying culinary acts. So even in the era of Peak Brisket, where it's more available than ever before, we hope this book will inspire you to get outside, light a chimney, and fire up some deliciously slow food.

—Jordan Mackay

1

—

OUT OF THE ASHES

Smokehouses, Storms, and Sauces

When it rains, it burns. Is that a saying? Maybe not, but I feel that I can say it after the time I've had since I last reported from the pages of *Franklin Barbecue* and *Franklin Steak*. While I've enjoyed my share of laughs and fun, now that I reflect on it, I've also had a stretch of struggles, just as you—and the country as a whole—surely have.

My wife, Stacy, and I are very lucky to have an incredible staff and loyal, loving customers who help to sustain us during challenging times. Nevertheless, I can easily imagine watching a zany Netflix series (like the oh so many we've binge-watched lately) based on the totally unpredictable developments that have occurred at Franklin Barbecue over the last seven years or so, including a fire in the middle of a rainstorm and the storm that is the COVID-19 pandemic. Cue a trailer featuring the high jinks surrounding a popular barbecue joint in never-a-dull-moment Texas. (I *do* wonder who the director would get to play Stacy.)

In many ways, this book has emerged out of the ashes, so to speak, after everyone's normal way of life broke down during the pandemic. Like many of you may have experienced, I found myself with more time at home than I'd had since I was a child. At first, when none of us knew how long the pandemic was going to last, I headed into the backyard where my grills, smokers, and firepits live and started cooking for my family. I'm lucky to be able to say that this strange situation turned out to be positive for a number of reasons: it was a reminder of what I love doing, an outlet for my creativity, and a good excuse to spend time outdoors. Soon enough, I found myself on Zoom meetings, doing video cooking demos, and generally shifting to a distanced online world. When I checked in with my coauthor, Jordan, he was going through a lot of the same stuff: tons of cooking and sort of reveling in the free time and space we suddenly had while trying not to worry too much about what was going to happen to life as we knew it.

But before we go there, let's rewind a few years so I can catch you up.

In 2017, we had a fire—a big fire. In what could be described as almost biblical circumstances—a driving wind and rainstorm powered by a massive hurricane hundreds of miles away—our smokehouse went up in flames. If the last thing you read about us was in *Franklin Barbecue*, you might have in mind the cowboy-like romance of how I cooked barbecue under the stars, espresso in hand, eyeglasses reflecting the flickering of a half-dozen roaring wood fires.

Well, that situation didn't last for more than a few years. In fact, the cover of *Franklin Barbecue* was photographed on the freshly poured concrete slab of what would become our new smokehouse. The main reason for building the smokehouse was both practical and legal. We didn't own the vacant dirt lot on which we had been cooking. We rented it. But our operation was spread between two separate properties, which, it turns out, isn't technically very legal. We had to combine operations into one property, a shift we had tried to make countless times. In the end, that wasn't possible.

So, we built the smokehouse. Its unusual design—a two-story addition to the existing restaurant, with an industrial elevator to haul firewood and meats from ground-floor storage to a second-floor room packed with crackling barbecue pits—reflected the necessities of our unique property. It is built into a surprisingly steep hillside on the edge of a commercial block and is the only smokehouse I've ever seen located on the second floor of a building. On paper, I admit, this is a terrible idea. But up in the air was the only place to put it.

Property lines were not the sole reason to build it, however. The smokehouse was also an attempt to make life easier for me and the other cooks. This was all part of our effort to step up and act like a real, sustainable business versus a collection of pieces jury-rigged together. You see, when we first opened the brick-and-mortar restaurant, we cooked out of the back lot by necessity. The setup was very rustic, making it feel as if we were still part food truck. While the restaurant that we took over had been a barbecue joint, the owner hadn't been cooking on offsets over live fire. Rather, he had two Southern Pride ovens, one he took and one he left behind. We had to cut out the back wall of the restaurant and get a slide truck in there to move that old oven out.

Late one night a few days before we were set to open, the inconvenient fact became clear that there was no place to put a couple of multi-thousand-pound barbecue pits. The only way we could set them up was to wheel the trailers right over. But that

was tricky because you can't have a door on one property, cross over to make food on a different property, and then cross back over to the original property to serve the hot food. Or at least you couldn't with our permits. That meant cooking in the back lot was a necessity. (And we rented that spot for $200 a month in, ahh, the old Austin of 2010.)

Two days before we opened, I cut a back door in the restaurant with a Sawzall to allow access to the vacant lot from our restaurant kitchen. Cutting through the metal on the side of the building was so dang loud. It was late at night, so Stacy was outside the wall with blankets trying to muffle the noise. Of course, at the time, most of the people sleeping in that neighborhood were the homeless or prostitutes and drug dealers—but we didn't want to wake them either!

There were no steps in the back lot, only gravel and dirt on the hillside—and it was slippery. When we had to add a new cooker to meet growing demand, I got railroad ties to terrace the hillside in order to fit more equipment. I'd be landscaping while cooking ribs. (Good thing a shovel is a multiuse tool.)

When we needed an office in our little shantytown, we added a trailer, which we still have. But, more important, we couldn't get a truck to unload firewood where we needed it, so it had to be hauled in. And there was no place to roll dollies, so briskets got dropped off on the front porch every day, and I had to pick them up and carry each box to the refrigerator. It was hard on the body and took a lot of time. I did the work because it was *our* business, but you can't expect to hire people for heavy loading when it's dark, dangerous, sometimes muddy or slippery, and completely brutal, physical labor.

I also hoped having a smokehouse that got us out of the rain, the wind, and the cold in winter would make our cooking more consistent. On the road to achieving that, though, the smokehouse made some aspects of our process *more* difficult. When I was cooking in the backyard, there was a little picnic table nearby where I could sit with my espresso. All the cookers were arranged so I could watch them at the same time—five or six at once. It was really convenient. Not so in the smokehouse. There was no vantage point from which you could see all the fires, so they had to be checked constantly. It took about a year, but we finally got our habits dialed in.

Back when I used to cook ribs, three degrees of temperature variability was my target. I might have one cooker at 278°F and the other at 275°F, burning really clean. That's not easy to do, and I was at the top of my game. When we moved into the smokehouse,

I had to relearn everything because all the radiant heat from the cookers got trapped in the room, making the ambient temperature hotter than it ever gets outside, even in the dog days of summer. And, of course, we had to extend the smokestacks enough to stick through the rooftop, which changed the dynamics of their draw. Plus, it was flippin' hot inside, just brutal—in the summer and in the winter.

Logistically, the smokehouse worked out great, and I was really happy with it, even if it slightly took away from the art of it all—but that's just me liking things as basic and as simple as possible. Altogether, it was a good thing. It made work less hard for people, which was the goal. (But the unintended consequence of *that* was that people didn't work *as* hard. Go figure.)

Now, the concept of building a wooden structure to hold several roaring fires might seem a little dubious. And, looking back, sure enough, it was.

The fire happened at around 5:00 a.m. on August 26. We close for about ten days every year in August to do maintenance and cleaning, and had saved up some money to put this amazing epoxy—the same stuff NASA uses—on the kitchen floor. I stayed at the closed restaurant while all the employees went on vacation. Then once we reopened, Stacy, our daughter, Vivian, and I took our vacation—the first time we had ever taken leave while the restaurant was open. I remember saying to the staff, "Alright, y'all, you got this! Don't mess it up. And don't call me unless the place is on fire." Talk about the dumbest thing I could possibly say.

Escaping Texas, we flew to Vermont, rented a car, drove to Montreal, and then headed down the Maine coast. We had a great time. On the night of the 25th, we were flying home from Portland, Maine. Hurricane Harvey, due to land that night on the Texas coast, was dominating the news. We were anxiously watching the TV, which was urgently broadcasting the news: "Texas Coast Braces for Harvey." Amazingly, our flight didn't get delayed. Nevertheless, with the reach of the coastal hurricane stretching all the way into Central Texas, we were warned that our flight might be a little dicey. Our approach was super-bumpy, and through the window I felt the clouds were blowing past at unnaturally fast rates. But we landed at 11:00 p.m. And after stopping for late-night tacos (of course!), we got home at midnight and poured ourselves into bed.

At 5:28 a.m., my phone started vibrating. The voice on the other end said, "Hey, the building's on fire!" I didn't freak out. I just said, "Okay, I'll be right there."

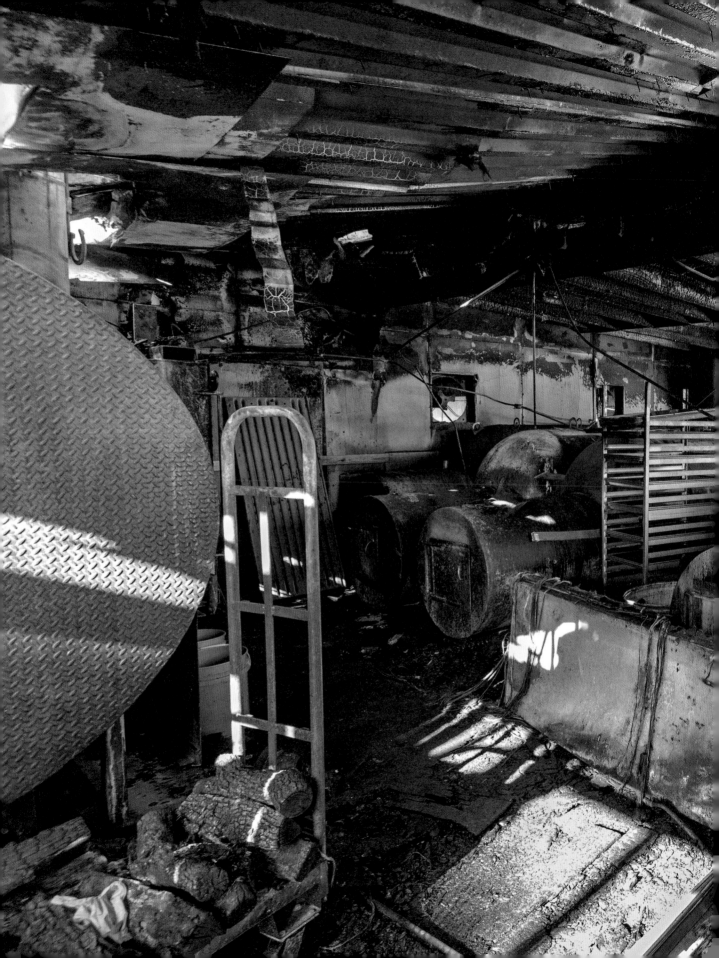

The fact is, I'd sorta been planning for this for a while. Like most kitchen people, I'm a prepper and had gamed a fire situation out in my mind. It seemed bound to happen one day. Hopefully it won't, I told myself, but if it does, I should definitely have my ducks in a row and not be caught off guard. So, I sat at the end of the bed for a second and collected my thoughts, then grabbed my shoes and slowly put them on, taking a deep breath. We'd been home for only six hours.

As I raced to the car, the weather was awful. The wind was howling, and sheets of rain were lashing the sides of my truck as I hit the highway in the pitch black of early morning. I got stuck at the interminable light at Twelfth Street with no other cars on the road, and I remember thinking, "Should I just run this?" Of course, I didn't, but from there I could already see the blue and red lights of the fire trucks reflecting off the clouds. Six or seven firehouses serviced the call, and the cops had arrived almost instantly. Everyone got there *so fast*. It makes me a little emotional just thinking about it.

At first, I didn't think it was going to be that bad—maybe just a wall or something. But when I arrived and found the whole street blocked off, cops and fire trucks everywhere, news vans already camped outside, the magnitude hit me. The cop at the roadblock just looked at me through my window, his expression downcast as he flagged me through saying, "Jeez, man, I'm so sorry." Everyone had their eyes on me as I walked up, eyeglasses dripping with rain. The devastation was shocking— walls burned out to the frames, ceilings crashed in, everything black and sooty. You wouldn't think that something could burn so heavy in a rainstorm. I went into the crowd and hugged the employees who were there. We were pretty shaken. Soon more employees, having seen the reports on the news, showed up.

Turns out the fire burned for just twenty-eight minutes, but, man, it did a lot of damage in that time. It started from Bethesda, the big, wood-burning rotisserie I had built. Due to the hurricane, that night had been really windy—windier than ever before. The smokehouse had screened-in windows but no storm covers. The wind came up from the ground floor, underneath the wood cage, and blew up through the elevator shaft to hit Bethesda's six-foot-long firebox. Our rib cook hadn't noticed that an ember had blown out of the firebox and tucked under a wall. It probably smoldered there for a few hours and, when more wind came through, the whole wall went up in flames all at once. Of course, at that point, the cook noticed and called 911. I'd installed some insulated heat shields and other things, but the wood in the walls had been heat-drying for a couple of years, making it extremely flammable. Later on, the firefighters told me it had gotten up to 1500°F in there.

In the end, we got real lucky because the outreach from our community was amazing. So many people called, texted, and emailed—we were flabbergasted. Someone from Europe saw the news on CNN and wrote in, completely worried and freaked out. Our restaurant burning down made international news? We couldn't believe it!

But, crucially, on that same day, the architect who'd helped design the smokehouse called, the framers reached out, the plumber checked in—everybody who had worked on the building. They said, "Hey, let us know when we can get started again." The general contractor said, "Tell me when, so I can clear my schedule." The city reached out almost immediately, and the permit guy that I'd dealt with on the first smokehouse said, "I can get this through pretty quick if you don't change much. I can resubmit the same plans and have a permit in your hand by the end of the week." It was like the plot of *The Blues Brothers*—we were getting the band back together!

The closure gave us a chance to make some improvements and take a much-needed break. Today, people note the unusual canted wall that juts out from the building at an angle far greater than 90 degrees. While, yes, that look does fit with my love of early modernist 1950s design, the reason for it is more practical. Let's just say that the smokehouse is something like 999.5 square feet. To go over a certain size would have pushed the project into an entirely different class of restaurant permitting, which would have been very difficult to navigate. The angled wall allowed us to fit in one more pit—a huge win for brisket capacity and for our ability to serve all our customers—with enough room for a cook to stand there and open the cooker door. We added steel window shutters so we can completely block the wind in case of another big storm. And we also changed the roofline—six feet on one side, four feet on another—and built a vent that allows the airflow to suck the radiant heat right out of the room.

To our great fortune, everything worked out. We maxed out every insurance policy—they all refused to renew our policies anyway—and began the rebuild. Construction lasted six months, but we were only closed for about three. When we first reopened, we were back to cooking outside. I had all new trailers built. We moved two of the cookers that we didn't like much from the smokehouse to use outside while we built two better replacements. Welcome, Mork and Mindy. Adios, Ciccone and MC5.

We reopened for business on the Tuesday of Thanksgiving week—a day that has mucho significance for us. It just happens that a lot of the same families come to the restaurant on that day every year. The amount of tears shed and number of hugs given as we walked up and down the line greeting people—talk about an emotional day. Who'd a thunk that barbecue could get people so worked up? That's when it dawned on me how much the restaurant means to so many people. And that's why we work so hard at what we do.

• • •

Lots of other stuff has happened in our little barbecue world since last I wrote. For a while, we had extra trailers in the parking lot to serve espresso and tacos. That was really cool. The coffee was primarily to cater to the people waiting in line for the restaurant, but people from all over the neighborhood ended up coming by too. And, not surprisingly, I drank my fair share. The taco truck was especially awesome because tacos are probably some of my favorite food. It was like a dream for me. We used brisket scraps, made our own delicious sauces, and even had eggs (which I don't like). The salsa was made with parsley (because I hate cilantro, a difficult situation down here in taco land). And the tacos were delicious. I loved it, and the truck was holding its own but, unfortunately, the pandemic shut it all down, and it didn't make the cut once we returned.

That said, today we have an awesome to-go trailer, which has been amazing for our business and our workflow. In true Franklin style, I bought a blank trailer and we customized it at the shop, adding prep and cutting stations, storage for to-go paraphernalia, a window, and so on. This operation is partly an evolution of a strategy to deal with the giant orders that often come from the head of the line. You see, the people who get in line early at the restaurant often come to place a huge order. But fulfilling those massive orders takes so much time, and it is agonizing to watch the faces of the rest of the folks who have been waiting almost as long and still have to sit by while we cut an insane amount of meat for just a handful of orders. So, we started diverting those big orders through the to-go trailer, which also services take-out orders and briskets for shipping. Right now, about half of our business goes through that trailer.

Having experience doing a solid to-go business and the fact that barbecue holds well for this kind of service were a real boon when the pandemic struck. As I said, I'm a prepper and don't like to be caught unaware. But the pandemic really caught me off guard! I don't keep up with the world of virology, and so I hadn't thought of this as a real possibility, much less gamed out situations if it did strike. Luckily, we had a leg up because we'd already started doing the to-go operation, which allowed us to transition quickly to pandemic conditions.

It was a Sunday in mid-March 2020. The South by Southwest conference had just been canceled, and an ominous feeling was settling over the world. No one was wearing masks in Austin yet, and it had become impossible to get people in our line to observe six feet of social distancing. So, Stacy and I just looked at each other and decided to close for dining and pivot to curbside service only. I don't know how Stacy did it, but within twenty-four hours, she had reconfigured the entire restaurant. We took out all the chairs and dining tables and moved in prep tables, coolers, and slicing stations. We brought in two computers, moved the telephone into the dining room, and figured out what we were going to offer, starting with minimum orders of three pounds. Stacy remade the website, figured out an ordering system, and photographed every item. By Monday, we had switched to curbside service. This was just a few days before the whole city shut down. Stacy has a photo of our sad, little darkened restaurant on a gray day in March with a sign out front reading

---

Dining Room Closed.

Curbside orders only. Franklinbbq.com.

We had no idea what to expect, but from the get-go, the curbside scene was *busy*. While Stacy, the brains of the operation, was inside directing the operation, I was outside managing traffic. Waiting cars started to back up, with the line stretching down the block. It was just like our usual lineup, only a car takes up a lot more space. Soon enough, the line was snaking down two blocks, curling around onto an arterial road, and even stretching onto the I-35 access road.

The city had to temporarily relocate a bus stop. I remember running around on foot, talking to people in cars on the access road, sounding ridiculous.

"Are you driving through or are you here for Franklin Barbecue?"

"I'm here for barbecue."

"Okay, head into this lane and just follow the car in front of you."

"Cool man. Hey, can I get a selfie with you?"

The pandemic was tough for everyone but it hit restaurants particularly hard. Yet, as things sort of stabilized, we realized that we could keep doing full to-go service, which kept us afloat during the long year and a half when we were closed for in-person dining. This allowed us to keep our heads above water, our workers employed, and our suppliers busy.

We even developed a healthy preorder business. Orders open six weeks in advance, exactly at midnight. You don't always have to plan that far ahead but should if it's Superbowl Sunday or Thanksgiving—all our orders sell out in about five minutes. However, if it's a Tuesday in the middle of winter, there's a good chance you could place an order only four days out. You still must order at least three days in advance so we can manage our quantities. After all, briskets take a half day to cook. And if people don't order it, we don't cook it.

We reopened the dining room to the public in the second year of the pandemic on, you guessed it, the Tuesday before Thanksgiving 2021. And, once again, just as when we opened after the fire in 2017, we saw many of the same people who make it a tradition to come on that day. Needless to say, it was another jubilant and emotional day.

• • •

I should also give y'all a heads-up about our new businesses. Some have been in the works for years, while others came about during the pandemic as ways of keeping us busy and challenged.

Over time, we had been getting tons of requests to ship our food, but due to capacity we were never able to satisfy that demand. During the pandemic, we were cooking less and were able to set some briskets aside to be chilled, shrink-wrapped, and shipped cross-country by Goldbelly or taken home by people who preordered them.

We're now starting to sell our sauces in bottles. I think our sauces are good, and we worked hard on them, but the idea of bottling occurred organically. It's not something we ever planned. And, indeed, it's been a very long process that Stacy has primarily directed.

We had been thinking about selling our bottled sauces, but the practicality it provided to our growing number of to-go customers made it a no-brainer. Once we began selling a ton of chilled, vacuum-sealed briskets—that people want to take on a plane or mail to friends—inserting an open pint of barbecue sauce became, well, messy. It sounds like a simple enough idea, but it suddenly became complex in execution. You can't just make sauce at a restaurant and put it into bottles. You have to use a certified manufacturer. And then once you get the sauce into a container, it must be shelf-stable and last for a certain amount of time. It also has to taste exactly the same as it does at the restaurant and live up to our standards of quality. That meant that the entire recipe had to be reformulated to account for all of this as well as increased production volume.

After many years of development in which we went through scores of recipe variations and tastings to ensure the bottled sauces tasted the same as the fresh ones, we were finally satisfied. (In fact, the new sauces are so good that we're using them in the restaurant now.) Then we had to figure out who was going to distribute the sauces, sell them, and where. Suddenly, a little idea that helped people who want to travel with a brisket became a brand-new business with a separate staff. Hopefully, these sauces will be coming to a store near you real soon because we're very proud of them and they taste good with *any* barbecue—not just ours. (By the way, we don't bottle our espresso sauce; it is only available at the restaurant. After years of trying, it turns out espresso is just too ephemeral to maintain consistency through bottling. Also, during the pandemic, as we honed our bottled sauces, I invented a new one: Spicy BBQ Sauce.)

We got rolling on another few businesses as well—charcoal, barbecue pits, rubs—which you can read about later in this book. These are items that we really wanted to have for ourselves and our friends and families and then thought maybe other people out there might also like to have them.

Well, that's a heck of an update. We're all breathing a little bit easier at Franklin Barbecue now. Who knows what the future will bring? No doubt its own share of calamity. But in the meantime, we have ever-greater confidence in our own abilities to cope and come through doing what we do best. And that's standing outside, tending a fire, and cooking up something good to eat, which is what the rest of this book is devoted to.

•   •   •

Franklin Smoke is a collection of ideas and recipes for using fire and smoke to cook everyday meals as well as a repository of dishes beyond barbecue that I've been preparing for years at special events and for family. A lot of what you'll find here is the kind of cooking Jordan and I do for ourselves and eat every day (surprise, it's not brisket!). We focus on getting the most out of a fire—in terms of process, flavor, and efficiency—over the entire life span of the coals, treating it not merely as a heat source but as an essential ingredient. We talk about smoking—and the offset cooker that I designed to get just the right touch of smoke flavor—and I detail my evolving thinking on smoking briskets. We break down some of the conceptual barriers that separate smoking and grilling, looking at the two as flip sides of the same coin: fire cooking. We offer techniques oriented toward the range of major cookers that most people have in their backyard. And we go deep into managing coal beds for different temperatures and durations to embrace a greater range of ingredients. As a result, I also include techniques for cooking some things that weren't included in my previous books, like vegetables, birds, fish and shellfish, and beef ribs. And, of course, meat plays a large role.

Along the way, you'll find ideas and some recipes for sides, sauces, and preparations and, as is expected, a detailed look at tools and equipment and serious talk about ideal setups. There is a bunch of recipes in here, too, but as usual, I don't distinguish between technique and recipe. I am way more into the former than the latter. I think if you figure out how to do something well—aka, learn the technique—then infinite recipes become available to you based on that knowledge. So, as always, do as I do and consider these recipes to be guidelines or formats to help you really learn the techniques.

2
—

THE HARDWARE

Smokers, Grills, and Firepits

Whether you're looking to smoke, grill, or do a little of both, you're going to need something to do it in. Given that myriad options exist in every category these days, selecting the right cooker is no easy task. The only question I probably get asked as often as "How do you know when to wrap a brisket?" is "What kind of smoker should I use?" And that question is almost unanswerable to me since I've cooked mostly on ones that I've built and used a few different styles here and there when I'm traveling. I've never tried too many of the hundreds of variations out there. That question is also one of the reasons—among others, as you'll see—that I decided to manufacture my own cookers. Now I have a surefire answer as to what I recommend.

Remember, you can always make a smoker out of a pit in the ground or a bunch of cinder blocks, and it'll cost you almost nothing. If you want to build a contraption big enough to smoke a whole hog and spend money on only a few big hunks of metal—steel bars, a steel plate for a lid, and maybe a burn barrel—you can do this on the cheap with a little bit of elbow grease. No, that pit will not be mobile, but if, say,

FRANKLIN SMOKE

you need to move houses, you could pretty easily disassemble it and build it again somewhere else. (Don't expect your grass to ever grow back. Sorry, Stacy!) And yes, this will live as a rather bulky structure in your backyard but, when it's not in use, it makes a fine surface on which to put your drink.

Similarly, instead of buying a fancy grill, you could always dump charcoal in a metal hotel pan, cover it with a cheap grate from a hardware store, and call it a grill—as my dad often did when I was a kid. Now, that's not going to give you any smoke unless you throw some wood chips on top, but it works for generating sizzle.

Likewise, you could spend money on a firepit (not to be confused with a barbecue "pit"), which I love, but remember that a firepit is just a convenient way to contain coals and fire, which could be made just as easily with a little indention in the ground surrounded by a circle of rocks.

You will not be surprised to learn that I believe the Texas-style offset smoker is the greatest device ever invented for cooking things with heat and smoke. While I am going to give some insight into how and why I developed my own smoker, your good use of this book is not at all contingent upon having one. And these techniques and recipes are certainly oriented toward offset cookers, but all the instructions can be applied or tailored to fit whatever type you have. And that includes the techniques of wood chopping and splitting, fire management, and cooking.

OFFSET SMOKERS

To avoid name confusion, I also use the word *pit* to mean a "smoker" or a "cooker," a relic from when folks roasted sides of beef or other large cuts over coals in a dugout trench in the ground. That's as rustic as it gets. To attain more control, enterprising cooks raised that pit off the ground, surrounded it with steel, moved the fire to one side, and exploited the remarkable phenomenon of airflow. Many people still call this a *pit* and some prefer to call it a *smoker*, but I often just refer to it as a *cooker*. So, I guess what I'm saying is that you can consider these terms interchangeable.

34

The Franklin Pit

For a couple of years, I had been producing and selling my own cookers on a miniature scale, but that started to ramp up recently. The challenge of designing a small backyard pit—as opposed to the bigger, longer ones that I and my crew weld for professionals—came up when I was writing my first book. Given that the construction of pits was so central to the narrative of *Franklin Barbecue*, and because I prefer to do it myself rather than pay someone, I decided to detail the steps to building a cooker in your backyard, as I did with my first homemade pit.

The plan had been to downsize a Franklin Barbecue professional pit for home use. We made the big pits from old propane tanks. However, the day that we went looking for a suitable tank, none could be found in the usual places. Instead, we bought big hunks of steel pipe, which were thicker and heavier than a propane tank, and made a cooker that both worked and was even pretty neat looking. I lit it up once or twice but never had time to really refine it. Today, it occupies a nice pedestal in the YETI flagship store in downtown Austin.

As time passed, the thought of creating personal pits never left my mind, and I've been working on the design for about six years now. The actual shape and form of the smoker is not terribly different from the rustic prototype; but to create a product like this, I learned that we also had to design the production methods and materials, figure out the economics, and create suitable systems for packaging and delivery. It was more complicated than I ever imagined, which is why it took so long before we had anything to sell. For the first couple of years, I was never entirely happy with the quality. We had to learn about tooling, fixturing, and achieving a good fit and finish. I wanted the pits to be perfectly round, which required rolling our own steel. And it took time to learn how to lathe the little fittings for the casters.

Originally, the production shop was housed at our little property in Bastrop, a small town outside of Austin. But it was naive of us to mount a commercial operation there, as we didn't have enough space, there was no loading dock, and we had limited storage. I had been thinking that we could put out two cookers a week, enough to keep a couple of welders working steadily. But those economics didn't work out. And I realized that if we were going to do this, we couldn't half-ass it. It couldn't be a hobby; it had to be a real business. So, we bought land and built a large facility in Austin, but we've already outgrown it. We also found production facilities that are far better at making the cookers than we ever could be in terms of precision, craftsmanship, and efficiency. The first of these refined and polished pits went on sale right at the beginning of the pandemic.

I've been through so many revisions of the design and seen it assembled in different forms and by different teams that I can honestly say that this is the best version of an offset smoker I can imagine. Applying the language of car engines doesn't feel inappropriate. Once you get a fire going in the cooker and see how it starts drawing air in and pumping smoke out through the stack, you'll think it revs like a hemi. And then, once it's up to speed, you'll enjoy how it handles—how one properly selected and placed log, a slight reconfiguration of the coal bed, or a subtle adjustment of the firebox door will reflect shockingly quickly in the temperature.

At a svelte six hundred eighty pounds, the Franklin Pit is truly a rudimentary sort of device whose only moving parts are two doors and the wheels it rolls on. It has no electrical cord, no engine, no fans. It runs on wood (or charcoal)—not pellets—and it doesn't connect to your phone, watch, or the internet. It is primitive technology crafted with contemporary precision and NASA-level materials. Many qualities separate this pit from the kind you can buy for a couple of hundred bucks (like the offset I started on) or even more. First, what makes this pit not only hard to build but also hard to package and ship is the weight of its materials. Most inexpensive or mass-produced smokers are constructed from very thin metal, which has many drawbacks. With a fire crackling inside for hours, the cheap steel will quickly deteriorate. Ill-fitting doors and holes in the steel will negatively affect your cook and cause you to waste fuel.

For the Franklin Pit, we tested various thicknesses of high-quality American steel until we found the one that could withstand fire after fire without changing shape. That thickness assures heat retention at the levels we expect at the restaurant and offers such durability that you could hand this down to your children and grandchildren. Furthermore, in iteration after iteration, we tweaked the design to ensure incredible draw and airflow.

Our firebox is fairly big and double-walled. This allows a large enough fire to push sufficient heat through the cooker while giving you a measure of control. By locating the fire toward the front or back in the firebox, you can significantly raise or lower the amount of direct heat flowing through the cook chamber with the smoke. You can also use real logs in our firebox, not only charcoal and chunks or chips. I recommend cutting logs in nine- to ten-inch pieces; this thing is meant to run on wood.

The door has the Franklin logo cut out of it, an intentional move to allow airflow and ensure that you never accidentally kill your fire. The door can be closed to slow down the fire a bit or opened wide to let air stampede through. But it's really meant to be closed, as the vents are a safeguard against running a dirty fire (one that is starved for oxygen and smolders).

The cook space on the grate inside is big enough to hold three medium-size briskets, enough food for thirty-plus people. Cooking just two briskets is ideal, but the third can be accommodated by placing it closer to the firebox (though I'd recommend setting an obstacle, like a log or a metal plate near the opening from firebox to cook chamber, to block some of the direct heat).

The passage between the firebox and the chamber contains a heat deflector plate that also serves to agitate the incoming stream of air, creating chaotic airflow that constantly bathes the meat in smoke on all sides.

The cooking grate comes out for cleaning with a wire brush and for oiling. The cook-chamber lid has been precisely engineered to open smoothly and handle easily. (It doesn't hermetically seal, however, because we want a little inefficiency there, this allows some variation to give space for delicate meats.) Of course, a Tel-Tru thermometer—the best!—is included. It sits two inches above the grate (the geographical center of most briskets) to measure the temperature the food is experiencing, rather than getting a reading from high above it. Also provided is a pan to fill with water and a shelf on which to place it inside the cook chamber to add humidity.

A grease drain and bucket underneath catch the drippings. Part of your post-cook ritual should be cleaning the pit while it's still warm and then wiping it down with oil. See Maintain Your Smoker on page 41 for tips on care. Remember to season the grates with oil, as well.

Inside, underneath the stack, is our proprietary (patent pending!) smoke collector, a complex design that is mounted on an ellipsoidal head. It directs and concentrates the airflow on the way out, like a guiding star, ultimately streamlining the chaotically moving smoke and air, focusing it around the meat before speeding it on its way.

The detachable smokestack is super-easy to affix: just stand it on its mooring and tighten the included bolts. The stack is a crucial part because it must be tall enough to have a meaningful impact. Air can't be pushed onto a fire efficiently—it must be

pulled. For that reason, we engineered the smokestack in reverse, starting with the stack and determining the ideal height and width to achieve perfect airflow. And, boy, does it draw, producing a powerful flow of clean smoke swirling in the chamber. Ultimately, forty-two inches turned out to be the magic number, which exactly mirrors the length of the cook chamber in a pleasing display of symmetry.

So, there you have the Franklin Pit as well as a mini-disquisition on the construction of offset smokers. No other kind of cooker smokes as consistently well, can be controlled so precisely with nothing but wood and airflow, and burns so cleanly with such sweet smoke as an offset. To be sure, there are other well-made offset smokers out there, so I encourage you to shop around for one that suits you. Or you can always build one yourself!

MAINTAIN YOUR SMOKER

Although a well-made smoker is pretty much indestructible, nothing is sadder than one that has been left out to rust or forgotten for months and is caked with disgusting remnants of grease and food. I've cleaned out a few of those suckers in my day, and it's never fun. So make sure you periodically clean out your smoker on the inside—get rid of ash, coals, and grease that might have fallen into the bottom and brush off the grates. I take care of the outside of my cookers by rubbing them down periodically, when they're still warm, with leftover fat from cooking or even just some grapeseed oil. Do the same with the cook chamber grate. This not only keeps 'em looking nice and sharp but also protects them for the long haul.

GRILLS

If a modern-day pit barbecue is just a way of getting a hole off the ground, then a grill is just a method of lifting a cooking fire off the ground. A grill contains the fire, which gives you more control and means you don't have to stoop down while cooking (helpful for those of us with tired backs). With that in mind, I can say that we're definitely living in the golden age of the grill. You can find a million versions and pay as much or as little as you want, go no-frills or add all the bells and whistles.

Since this is a book about cooking over live coals, we're not going to talk about gas grills. While I don't personally use them, even I admit that they have some value if you're just looking to get a little char or some grill marks without any fuss or waiting. But I'm all about the fuss and waiting, often to the annoyance of my family!

In chapter 4, I talk about getting good smoke flavor from the grill, which is not always an easy thing. Charcoal doesn't provide much flavorful smoke on its own. Its action is more like that of a gas grill; the flavor comes from juices and fat dripping down from the ingredient to the heat source, vaporizing, and then rising back up to coat the food. This, on its own, is a distinctly sought-after and delicious flavor. So keep that in mind as you read about the various types of grills.

Kettle Grills

The standard kettle grill allows you to contain a charcoal bed, control the air feed from underneath, and trap heat and smoke with a big domed lid. Its geometry is brilliant, allowing you to have a small heat source in relation to a relatively large cooking area. It is inexpensive and easy to wheel around a deck or driveway. You could even keep a smaller one on an apartment balcony. While a kettle grill works well enough for straight grilling, it has some limitations.

One of those limits is flexibility. True two-zone cooking is compromised. When the cooking zone sits directly over the heat source, you don't have a lot of room to operate away from the heat (and some of the heat from the hot zone inevitably leaks over to the cool zone). A kettle grill is good for a sear and direct cooking but not ideal for more nuanced techniques.

The ability to smoke is also limited on this grill. The lid helps you contain heat and vapor, but a lot of that vapor is actually charcoal fumes, which are not the best. If you push all the coals to one side, you can create a makeshift two-zone setup and add some wood chips or chunks to create smoke, but the airflow isn't great. The vertical distance the smoke travels from the heat source to the top vent is short and direct and lacks proper pull—and the smoke from a smoldering fire is usually not very sweet—so it's hard to get a full, clean cook.

Finally, kettle grills are inexpensive because the metal used to make them is thin. On one hand, that makes them highly portable and affordable. On the other hand, that super-thin metal means it has a limited life span and just leaks heat, which makes it difficult to keep temperatures up for more than twenty to thirty minutes. During longer smokes or roasts, you must add new charcoal often, which is a pain and also slows the cook.

An old kettle grill can be useful for quick, hot cooks and as a place to burn down logs into a steady supply of wood coals that can then be transferred to any sort of cooker to which you don't want to add charcoal. A cheap kettle grill is a mighty handy thing, no doubt, but we can also do better.

PK Grills

I expounded on my affection for the PK (Portable Kitchen) Grill in my second book, *Franklin Steak*. In the intervening years, the company has released some exciting new models. My relationship with the company also progressed, as they allowed me to offer some tweaks and suggestions for their classic grill, which became a whole new model, the PK300AF.

PK is a brand from the early 1950s that had a loyal following until the company went through some trials and tribulations and eventually ceased production. One of those loyal followers rediscovered it in the mid-1980s and decided to resurrect the brand. I found it years ago and used it for all my grilling. I love not only the 1950s space-age look but the masterful construction and design. An oblong shape allows for true two-zone cooking. Four adjustable vents, two on top and two underneath, provide airflow control like no other charcoal grill has. The coal bed is positioned right up close to the grill, allowing for efficient use of charcoal and super-hot searing. And thick aluminum construction holds heat incredibly well (making it suitable for longer cooks) and conducts heat four times better than steel. It is also rust- and dent-resistant and will last for generations. On top of all this, it's not so heavy that one person can't lift it, it's easy to clean, and it's pretty darn portable. Creating a product that will outlive the buyer in our world of planned obsolescence might not be a business model that Wall Street sharks would approve of, but it's the kind of thing I love and support.

The PK is obviously great for grilling and the favorite of many steak cook-off champions in recent years because of its ability to create intense, direct heat. But it can also be used as a smoker, as its shape and vent design allow you to crudely mimic the action of an offset smoker.

The PK model that I used for years and years is called the Original. I loved it so much that I touted it to anyone who asked (it's rare for me to "tout" anything) and recommended that all my grill-shopping friends consider it. Thanks to this unsolicited enthusiasm, the company brass and I ended up becoming friends, which is how a few of my ideas became incorporated into the PK300AF. The 300 indicates three hundred square inches of cook space, while the AF indicates . . . well, you get it.

The PK300AF is basically a redesigned Original with thoroughly considered new details and a few major additions—elements that, over years of cooking on it, I realized would make the experience just a little bit better. In fact, PK recently updated the Original model, too, incorporating several features such as radial top and bottom vents, which are more precise and easier to manipulate; a better hinge; an upgraded ash control system inside the cooker; a collapsible work surface; and an improved cart. The AF additions are practical and cosmetic, including a little rack on which to hang towels or tongs or whatever you want (they call it a "belly bar"); one more collapsible work surface, doubling the amount of space; and speed racks built right into the cart that hold standard-size sheet pans for added shelf space (the top one even gets warmth from the bottom of the grill). Finally, the PK300AF comes in the bright teal of Franklin Barbecue or in coal-black with teal flakes.

Although I've always clung to the Original model out of aesthetics and habit, the PK360, which PK calls its flagship model, is a great grill too. Its larger form factor provides an additional sixty square inches of grill space, which come in handy. The construction is super-solid, with two winged shelves for placing all your ingredients (and your beverage). And the knobs that PK created for controlling the air vents on the bottom are much more convenient to use than the knobs on the other models, which are located underneath.

The PKGO is a nifty little device that's way more than a hibachi. It's incredibly light, portable, and nice for all manner of single-zone grilling, but with its dual vents, lid, and shape, it actually offers two legit zones. It's also small enough to cart along in the trunk of your car, which is what I do on long, solo road trips.

Santa Maria–Style Grills

A Santa Maria is the type of grill that has a broad, flat surface to hold a thin layer of coals and a grill grate attached to chains and cranks that can be lowered up and down to the desired height above the heat.

The ability to control the distance between the coals and grate allows for real delicacy and finesse in how you cook something. It's just elevated (pun intended) firepit cooking. You can take, say, a heavier piece of meat (like the tri-tip steak that people in Santa Maria, California, are famous for cooking) and sear it with some up-close heat before raising it to collect gentler heat and some smoke as it cooks all the way through with precision. The crank action allows you to easily replenish the hot coals, making it ideal for use in restaurants or for large gatherings when you've got waves of food to put out. Plus, it looks cool!

Kamado Grills

The ferocity of love, loyalty, and affection that people feel for their kamado grills never ceases to amaze me. Not that these tools aren't worthy of appreciation. It's just that the people who get into them, really get into them! The great appeal of a kamado, such as the Big Green Egg, lies in its versatility and ability to achieve and hold a steady temperature over a long period of time—two of the greatest challenges of cooking barbecue. Because of this, you can roast, bake, and do some degree of smoking on it.

Based on a Japanese design, these cookers are both heavy and bulky thanks to their thick, dense ceramic construction. That means once you put your kamado somewhere, you probably won't want (or be able) to move it. Due to the shape of the grill and the material, the coals are directly underneath the grate. Big Green Egg makes EGGcessories (as they call them), including one that allows you to sequester the coals on one side for a two-zone setup. That might shield food from direct heat but, when you close the lid, the oven-like effect can make it extremely hot inside. I think it works best to stabilize the temperature before grilling. That can take a long time, however, and if you start with too much heat in the first place, cooling down can take a while once this grill gets rolling. It's why practicing on your specific grill is so key. Big Green Egg also makes a heat-shielding plate, which is helpful for smoking. It sits directly underneath your food and forces the smoke up and around into the chamber while also deflecting some of the direct heat. You can get some reasonable smoke in this situation, though it doesn't provide the draw, convection, and clean smoke of a good offset smoker.

COLD EGGS

While Aaron and I were working on this book, I moved across country from California to the icy Northeast. It was my first real East Coast winter, and, despite what people from Wisconsin had told me about grilling year-round, it was definitely hard to get outside and get fires going when our driveway and yard were covered in ice and snow for weeks at a time. However, the few times that I was able to carve a little space to wheel a cooker out of the garage onto the drive, the Big Green Egg proved to be a good adversary against subfreezing temperatures. It heated up well and bravely held its warmth in the cold. —**Jordan**

FIREPITS

Firepits are like labradoodles—they're everywhere these days! Realtors love to photograph houses with a happy family laughing in front of a firepit as the flames and embers dance up into the night sky. Of course, nature's original firepit is as basic as the name suggests. Not only are they primordial (and naturally occurring, sometimes) but firepits, whether in a campsite or a backyard, connect us all. Campfires are the preindustrial televisions! They're nice for ambience, but I appreciate their utility as well. And now there's a new wave of high-end firepits that come with various attached cooking apparatuses that make them even more functional.

A number of years ago, I built a good-size firepit for my family, and we use it often. At the time, we lived in a house without a lot of backyard space, so it was nice to have a contained space for a fire on the back patio. Ours is quite large; made of solid steel, it is four feet in diameter and almost two feet high. The size allows for a very large fire and for five or six people to sit comfortably around it. Welded to the bottom and elevated a few inches above the ground is an external ring that runs around the circumference, serving as a handy footrest. After an hour or so, your toesies get nice and hot resting on the rail, even on the coldest nights. There's also a semicircular grate, which makes it perfect for campfire cooking. It's nothing fancy, but it provides a large surface on which to grill while offering full access to the fire itself to add logs and to push coals around.

Another use for a firepit is as a side fire to produce a ready supply of fresh wood coals that can then be used instead of charcoal in any grill.

3

—

THE WOODSHED

A Prime Ingredient and Other Fuels

Where there's smoke, there may be fire. But where there's barbecue smoke, there better be wood. The soul of barbecue is wood. You could argue that it is barbecue's entire reason for being. Not to wax too poetic or anything, but wood is also what connects us to the land, to our natural environment, and to our own deep history as humans and animals. From a materials science point of view, wood is a truly incredible substance as well, designed by nature to be almost as strong, in certain cases, as stone or metal, yet also cuttable, penetrable, and burnable.

I still spend a fair bit of my time loading and unloading firewood from the back of my truck, whether I'm bringing home logs for a backyard cook, schlepping wood to an event, or setting off into nature for a camping trip. It never feels like a chore.

When it comes to cooking, wood is all the rage these days. In outdoor fire cooking, I consider wood to be the prime ingredient. And the quality of the wood is one of the most underappreciated aspects of smoking, which surprises me because wood provides a huge part of the food's flavor. The quality of the combustion of the wood has everything to do with how your food cooks and tastes. With that in mind, I suggest you pay attention to where your wood comes from and its size, consistency, and seasoning level. Of course, wood is a natural, organic product, so you can't expect perfect uniformity from one log to the other. But, in general, you want to have confidence in your supply and to pay attention to each piece you throw on the fire.

In addition to wood, I discuss charcoal in this chapter. Charcoal is valuable to me as a heat source, but I mostly use it in conjunction with wood. As the only true fundamentals of fire cooking, both these elements are worth understanding.

The amount of information—and opinions—about wood for barbecue has exploded in recent years. In some ways, I think the discussions have gotten out of hand. People who are just getting started with barbecue ask me all the time what I think about this or that kind of wood. And while I have had great experiences cooking on all sorts, I would be remiss not to admit that the vast majority of my cooking is done with the wood that is widely available in my area: good ol' Central Texas post oak. While I love post oak, I don't necessarily value it higher than any other kind of suitable barbecue wood. In other words, there's great worth in getting to know the primary wood in your area really well—how it cooks, how it tastes, how it feels. If you want to check out other woods, by all means, play around. But it's good to have a steady companion in barbecue. That said, there are a couple of rules you want to keep in mind.

HARDWOODS VERSUS SOFTWOODS

I like all kinds of wood for cooking as long as they are well seasoned and sourced. The only ironclad rule is that it be a hardwood. That is, don't use softwoods such as leftover IKEA furniture or pine or cedar or fir. Not only do softwoods go up like torches, but they're also commonly full of resins and compounds called terpenes. The smoke from these woods often smells pungently herbal and piney, and so will your food if you use them. Plus, these woods burn so hot and fast that it becomes difficult to control the fire.

Hardwoods, like oak, hickory, almond, pecan, and fruitwoods (apple, cherry, pear), all burn consistently and less wildly and have a deliciously savory smoke. Unlike the compounds of softwoods, the compounds of hardwoods include lignin and flavonoids, which break down through combustion into sweeter- and spicier-smelling smoke.

Just because wood is labeled "hardwood" doesn't always mean it's harder than a wood labeled "softwood." Balsa, for instance, which is often used in model-ship construction, is a very, very soft hardwood. Aspen and alder are both quite soft hardwoods too. On the other hand, southern pine is one of the heaviest, most durable softwoods.

While the terms *hardwood* and *softwood* stem from the descriptions that colonists gave to the woods they used for building, the difference between the two is more technical. Hardwoods have broad leaves, are angiosperms (reproduce by fruit and flower), and are often deciduous, which means they lose their leaves for a time each year. Softwoods, in contrast, are gymnosperms, meaning they reproduce by unencased seeds (not surrounded by a fruit or nut).

Practically speaking, the major differences relate to structure, grain, and content. Softwoods transport moisture, often in the form of resinous sap, through longer, tubelike ducts that make them feel softer when cut. Hardwoods move moisture through shorter, rounder pores of various diameters. When you cut into them, they feel much more solid. People often identify various woods by looking at magnified pictures of crosscuts to examine the pore structure.

Much as there's a measurement of the heat levels in chiles (the Scoville scale), there's a test for hardness in wood, known as the Janka hardness test. Although it sounds like a bar game and does involve shooting a metal ball, it's named for Austrian emigrant Gabriel Janka, a wood researcher who developed the test in 1906. It measures the amount of force needed to embed that steel ball halfway into a six-by-two-by-two-inch piece of wood.

The hardest woods are tropical hardwoods. Australian buloke (a species of appropriately named ironwood) takes the crown with a whopping 5,060 pounds-force (lbf). For reference, live oak checks in at 2,380, mesquite at 2,345, sugar maple at 1,450, and cherry at 995. My beloved post oak is a comfortable 1,350, similar to many other kinds of oak. By comparison, Douglas fir, a softwood, scores 660, while several pines are under 450. Janka measurements are more applicable to using wood as a building material than for barbecue, but it's still good to know something about the materials in your fire.

CHOOSE YOUR WOODS WISELY

Naturally, I'm 100 percent devoted to post oak, which burns sweet, hot, and clean. Of course, there are tons of other kinds of wood. You may read about people who choose certain types for various foods. And while that's all fine, I personally wouldn't fret about the kind of wood as long as it's a hardwood and it's well seasoned. There are differences, but you may not notice them unless you cook with one type all the time and then suddenly change. Your ability to deploy wood and fire is far more important than the flavor of each individual species of tree. That said, one thing I don't like to do at all is to mix woods on the same cook. To my mind, it muddies the palate.

A very useful article posted by the Forest Products Laboratory of the US Department of Agriculture notes that "the chemical composition of wood cannot be defined precisely for a given tree species or even for a given tree. Chemical composition varies with tree part (root, stem, or branch), type of wood (i.e., normal, tension, or compression), geographic location, climate, and soil conditions." So whether you're burning cherry or apple or maple, the flavor donated by a chunk or log depends less on the species and more on where it grew and what part of the tree it came from. If you're buying a box or bag of applewood chunks, you know what kind of wood it is (or at least, how it has been labeled), but you rarely know where it came from.

That's why I recommend you use what grows around you and you can get from a good local source. Post oak tends to give an even, mellow, and sweet flavor and burns quite well. Hickory burns as well as oak, but its flavor can be a bit more aggressive. I like the mild flavor of well-seasoned pecan and almond. And unlike many people, I'm not too put off by mesquite. While it can burn very hot and fast, almost like a softwood, and can have an aggressive flavor, I like the way it tastes on the grill when it's well seasoned, and it can give good flavor to a long smoke. Cherry is also quite distinctive, with a high-toned sweet, fruity aroma and a smoke that imparts a distinctive reddish hue to whatever's bathed in it, which makes it popular in competition barbecue.

'Tis the Season

Well-seasoned firewood is essential to a good smoke. Not every piece of wood in your fire has to be perfectly air-dried for two years—there is a time and place for denser logs. What you want to avoid is very green wood, aka wood from a tree that's been cut down recently. When I talk about green wood versus seasoned wood, what's really an issue is water content.

Unsurprisingly, the more water in a log, the worse it burns. That's because the heat from the fire must evaporate the water inside the wood before it can burn the remaining cellulose as a fuel source. Evaporating water—turning it from liquid to vapor—takes a great deal of energy. In fact, turning boiling water into steam takes five times the amount of energy required to bring that same amount of water from freezing to boiling. So, when your fire is trying to vaporize all that water, huge amounts of precious energy are being spent. This results in incomplete combustion, which creates heavy, wet smoke filled with creosote and other compounds that you definitely do not want to have clinging to your food. Have you ever eaten smoked food with a bitter aftertaste? That's bad smoke from a choked-off fire. Properly seasoned wood that is properly combusted solves that problem.

I don't use wood chips—or even wood chunks—but I still get asked whether they should be soaked before use. (The idea is that inundating the wood with water will keep it from bursting into flames when you put it on top of charcoal to get some smoke on your food.) I hope by now that you can anticipate my answer. This is a terrible idea for a couple of reasons. First, wet wood will always take energy out of your fire or your coals. Second, the quality of smoke from smoldering wet wood chips is not desirable. Indeed, it is what I usually call steam. Use dry wood.

It's shocking how much water can be carried within the cells of a piece of wood. Moisture content is measured as a percentage equal to the weight of the water in the wood divided by the dry weight of the wood times one hundred. You can technically have fresh pieces of wood with a moisture content of more than 100 percent when the water weighs more than the wood. Seriously, a very heavy piece of green firewood could contain a half gallon of water. You definitely don't want to try starting a fire with this wood, as it would be almost impossible to get it going.

One way to measure moisture content is with a moisture meter, a little battery-powered device with two pins you stick into a piece of wood, which can be bought inexpensively at a hardware store or online. The ideal moisture content for cooking wood is between 15 and 25 percent. A very hot coal bed in the firebox can absorb more water-laden logs, but keep in mind what you throw on there—even a raging fire will struggle when fed overly damp wood.

The easiest way to estimate moisture content in wood is with a version of the traditional touch test. The touch test won't give you an exact percentage, but it'll tell you enough about the log in question to be able to make a "seasoned" judgment (see Sensing Firewood, below).

Now, I haven't been the biggest fan of kiln-dried wood in the past, mostly because it was always dried to such a low moisture content that it burned too fast to cook effectively and had little flavor. Also, a lot of what's being sold as boxed firewood in local stores is pine or another softwood, so be careful. I wouldn't even use those in my fireplace, let alone my smoker. However, you can find some kiln-dried hardwood firewood that falls within the moderate-moisture-content sweet spot—again, between 15 and 25 percent—that works just fine in a smoker. This approach is more expensive than buying wood in bulk from a local supplier and then aging it yourself, but it works well enough. Also, I've found that kiln-dried chunks can work very well in small smokers or in conjunction with charcoal in a kettle grill, PK grill, or Big Green Egg.

SENSING FIREWOOD

Picking the perfect log to throw onto the fire is easy if you know what you're looking for. You will employ multiple senses while doing this.

TOUCH Pick up a few logs individually and compare their weight. If one is very heavy, as if made from stone, it's still green and contains a lot of moisture. That one's a candidate for more seasoning. If a log is really light or feels about average, it's likely well seasoned and you can use it with impunity—to start a fire from scratch or to keep a good fire truckin' along.

SIGHT Note the color of the log. Really well-seasoned wood turns gray. If you go to Lockhart, Texas, and check out the giant wood yard for big BBQ restaurants, like Kreuz or Smitty's, you'll find a lot of neatly stacked gray logs. You can tell that stuff has been sitting out for a couple of years and is really seasoned and dry. Also, well-seasoned wood tends to crack and shed its bark as it gets to a good place. If the wood still has a lot of color, be it yellowish orange, like fresh wood, or greenish, you know it's not seasoned enough. Fresh wood looks like a pristine log.

SOUND Tap two pieces of firewood together or tap the log in question against a stone. If you hear a heavy, muted clunk, you're probably holding a big, water-laden piece of improperly seasoned wood. If it offers a slightly resonant, hollow thump, it's good to go.

To season your own wood, stack it so the cut ends of the logs are facing out. The logs respirate, so to speak, through the pores bared at the cut ends—it's where moisture evaporates—so you want them exposed to as much airflow as possible. Likewise, unless it's raining directly on your woodpile, don't cover your wood with a tarp. Air movement is the key to evaporation, and if the logs are smothered underneath a big piece of plastic, they'll take much longer to season. The best woodpiles are stacked under roofed, open-sided sheds.

Log Size

When you buy firewood by the cord or some fraction of a cord, it tends to come in lengths of fourteen to eighteen inches. Sometimes you might get really fat logs or logs that are too long. Often the size of your logs needs to be altered—for your home fireplace and especially for cooking.

Every cooker has its preferred fire size. And every fire has its preferred wood size. Your job is to match wood to fire to cooker. For the Franklin Pit—and for most smaller offset smokers—logs in the nine- to ten-inch range fit perfectly into the firebox. While a standard-size log will technically fit into the twenty-four-inch-long firebox of a Franklin Pit, it's too big to burn effectively. Its bulk will restrict airflow and remove a lot of energy from the fire as it catches. And when it does start to burn, it's going to send your temps through the roof. Smaller logs are easy enough to fashion from the big ones. In fact, it's never a bad thing to keep some more modestly sized firewood on hand. It's good for getting fires started and for building smaller fires in, say, a kettle grill.

If you're cooking on a large firepit or in an indoor fireplace, you can certainly get away with full-size logs. The size of your cooker will clearly tell you what size wood you need. And be sure to have plenty of wood in the needed size to last through the length of your cook. You don't want to have to cut more once you've started cooking.

Experience and practice will teach you the best size log for your cooker. It becomes obvious rather quickly when, say, a log that's too big takes a long time to catch and, in the process, sucks the energy of your fire. Or when a log that's too small flames up immediately and disappears before it's made much of a contribution to the cook. A bit more questionable are logs that are just slightly too large and dense. They may catch quickly but then provide too big a boost of heat. You'll learn rapidly just

by watching the firebox and the thermometer to gauge the impact of each particular log. And remember, it's perfectly fine to pull a log off if it's giving too much heat or taking away from your fire.

WOOD TOOLS

Wood handling is an important part of cooking barbecue of any kind. If you're dealing with wood fires, though, wood management is more complex than just throwing another log onto the fire. Sometimes your wood needs to be resized, split, or splintered to maximize its benefits. Here are the tools you want to have around to get the most out of your fires.

WORK GLOVES It's always good to have a pair of these handy! Seriously, if you're like me and constantly hauling around firewood in the back of your truck, loading it here, unloading it there, you're going to want a pair of lightweight work gloves (canvas, Kevlar, or polyester will work) to avoid all those pesky splinters.

SAWS To trim my firewood down from eighteen inches to a more workable nine or ten inches, I use a chop saw (aka miter saw), but you can technically use any kind of saw you want or have. I have a chop saw mounted in my shed because I'm always building something or working on the house. It's really meant for cutting lumber or molding, but it works well for firewood too. It's the kind with a sharp-toothed saw wheel that spins on an arm you raise and lower to cut through the wood, which is anchored in place. It's really fast (and kind of dangerous, so remember to always work safely).

I saw each big log to about two-thirds of its length, or approximately ten inches. If you are using a chop saw, be sure to secure the log tightly between the saw's grips. Firewood doesn't have flush edges, like lumber, so be extra careful when bringing the sawblade down that it doesn't twist or catch the wood and toss it off somewhere or pull your hand in. Make fast, decisive motions when dropping the blade for the cut and raise it back up quickly.

If you don't have a mounted stationary saw, you can use a chainsaw or a reciprocating saw, like a Sawzall, which is often used for cutting tree branches. Just be sure you have a wood blade for your reciprocating saw (they have fewer teeth than blades intended for cutting metal). The main danger with all types of saws is kickback, so you must anchor your wood securely. (And, hey, if you want the exercise, a good old-fashioned handsaw works too!)

Trimming down your wood should obviously be done at the beginning of a cook. Cut as much as you think you'll need, because once you've opened that first beer or mixed that first cocktail, razor-sharp power tools have no place in your life.

MAUL Most firewood comes pre-split, but it's rarely the exact size you need. Matching the width of the wood to the size of your fire (and cooker) is as important as matching the length. Doing so is a knack that comes with both practice and intuition, but it's not as mysterious as it sounds. If you have a small or medium fire, it's easy to see that putting a massive log on it will destroy its momentum for the span of time it takes that log to catch (if it doesn't extinguish your fire altogether). So what do you do? You split a big, fat piece into two, three, or four smaller ones. I do this dozens of times a day using a maul.

If a sledgehammer and an axe had a kid, it would be a maul, which sports the blunt heaviness of the former and the general look and shape of the latter. Whereas axes are used to splinter and slice wood largely against the grain, a maul is used with the grain. It divides the wood where it wants to split naturally. Mauls come in all manner of weights, so choose one that you can swing and control without laboring (mine has an eight-pound head).

The maul can be used in two ways: you strike the wood directly with the V-shaped, axe-like edge to split it, or you use the dull, sledgehammer-like side in conjunction with a separate metal wedge. The wedge adds another step, but if you tap it into the grain of the wood where you want the split to occur and then pound it with the sledge, you achieve greater accuracy.

I skip that part, though, and just go directly into the wood. First, you need to find a good chopping block on which to stand the log on its end (or a solid patch of flat ground). Stand back an appropriate distance and distribute your weight across your shoulder-width-spread feet. Focus your eyes on a line of the grain that runs from the outside of the wood to the center. Raise the maul and bring it down decisively, keeping your eyes on the spot you want to hit. Don't try to swing it down hard. The point of the heavy head is to let gravity do most of the work for you. You should do some damage on the first swing, but if the log doesn't split all the way through, give it a second try, and even a third, in the same spot, and you'll hear that satisfying sound of cleaving wood fibers as the perfectly sized split falls to the ground.

HATCHET Once you've created some smaller logs, you may also want to split off some kindling to help get your fire started. For this, a hatchet, the short-handled form of an axe, is a useful tool. Although it's not powerful enough to split a full-size log, it does offer the benefit of control, which is an important aspect of safety. Just place your little log on a stump or other flat surface. Make sure it can stand on its own end, as you never want to put your free hand on the log you're about to split. Then just make a decisive chop along the grain somewhere close to the edge of the log. You may have to hit it a couple of times to get a smaller sticklike piece seven to ten inches long and an inch or less in width. But with a little effort, it's not hard to generate the four or five pieces you need to get your fire started.

STORE-BOUGHT WOOD CHUNKS

As Aaron has mentioned, he's not a big fan of the bags of wood chunks you can buy at the store, but he lives a charmed life around a constant source of seasoned firewood. I've had good success getting flavorful smoke from store-bought kiln-dried wood chunks. While I disregard those labeled "cherry" or "hickory" (I usually opt for oak), when it's nestled atop a pile of thoroughly heated charcoal in a PK grill, a fat chunk of wood—even kiln-dried!—can give a good half hour of smoke. A moisture-meter reading on some wood chunks revealed 8 percent water content, which is a bit dry for optimal smoking. They are no substitute for a real wood fire and not a great solution for doing a long cook, like brisket, but for smaller things, they work quite well. —**Jordan**

CHARCOAL

Recently, I've had the adventure of helping to create our own brand of charcoal, and I've learned a lot. Since I've been cooking barbecue, I have to admit that I haven't been a big charcoal guy. Nothing, in my mind, can substitute for the coals achieved by burning down actual wood. However, now that I've been around charcoal more, I've softened a bit on its value.

Good charcoal sure is handy when you don't have time to build a full and proper coal bed out of wood or when you just need a quick, consistent form of intense heat. In fact, charcoal has a lot going for it, and humans have been making it and using it for more than thirty-eight thousand years. This is backed up in "The Art, Science, and

Technology of Charcoal Production," a 2003 paper by two experts in the study of renewable energy resources that observes, "As a renewable fuel, charcoal has many attractive features: it contains virtually no sulfur or mercury and is low in nitrogen and ash; it is highly reactive yet easy to store and handle." It becomes a lot easier to make choices about charcoal—briquettes or lump? mesquite or coconut?—when you understand a bit about where it came from.

Charcoal is nothing more than wood that has been cooked for days in a low-oxygen environment. Primitive humans learned that they could create charcoal by burying smoldering wood underground or covering it in a mound with heavy earth or clay. Modern humans do the same thing in industrial silos or burn chambers. The lack of oxygen keeps the wood from burning completely but generates enough heat to burn off most of the volatile compounds that existed in the original wood, including water, tar, hydrogen, methane, and more. What's left at the end are black chunks and fine powder made almost completely of carbon and some minerals and other impurities that don't burn away.

Charcoal ends up being about one-fourth the weight of the wood it was made from and burns far hotter when lit, thanks to the absence of all those volatiles. This makes it truly valuable as a heat source, though not at all valuable as a flavor source. All the organic and volatile compounds that were burned off during the production process are what makes woodsmoke aromatically compelling. Without that, you just have something that burns very hot, long, and (relatively) clean.

Depending on what kind of charcoal you're using, it may give off some fumes, sparks, and smoke when first lit. None of this is desirable for cooking, which I'm sure I don't need to tell you. But once it gets going, it burns very clean with little smoke and little impact on aromatics. What we taste as charcoal-grill flavor is very similar to the grill flavor from a gas grill. It's the ignition of the oils and juices—the fats, rubs, marinades, and so on—dripping from whatever you're cooking onto the heat source. Once they hit, they quickly vaporize and rise up to bathe the food in what amounts to a little smoky cloud of its own substance. The rest of the grill flavor comes from the Maillard reaction (browning)—represented by grill marks—that happens on the surface of the food thanks to heat and searing.

Briquettes versus Lump Charcoal

The big question on most people's minds when shopping for charcoal is whether to go for briquettes or lump. If you want to understand anything about charcoal, this is a good place to start. But before I say a word on the subject, I want to note that I'm speaking in general terms here. Every brand of charcoal is different, so it's hard to make definitive statements on this subject. That said, here's my general thinking on the matter of briquettes versus lump charcoal.

Charcoal briquettes are made from scrap wood and especially sawdust collected in giant quantities from such places as sawmills. At a charcoal plant, larger pieces of wood or foreign matter, like metal or rock, are separated out before the wood particles are dried and then carbonized (cooked until they are mostly just pure carbon). This carbon powder is then collected, potentially blended with other ingredients, dried, and stamped into briquettes. Those other ingredients may include anthracite coal (which helps the briquettes burn hotter and longer), limestone (which helps them turn white so you know when to start cooking), cornstarch (a binder), and nitrate (to speed up ignition). But I'm told by friends who know the industry that some of these additives are blended into the mix because wood is expensive, and it's cheaper to add external forms of coal than actual wood.

So if you don't like the sound of these additives in your fuel source—I don't—look for all-natural charcoal that has almost nothing added. This is exactly what I did and how I ultimately decided to make my own out of Texas post oak. To my knowledge, there's no other exclusive post oak charcoal out there. Our Franklin briquettes are made from nothing but post oak pieces, charcoal "fines" (the fine dust and other particles left from post oak handling), and a very small amount of vegetable starch as the binder, just as bread crumbs help to hold a meatball together. I've been nothing short of impressed with how hot and long they burn. And they don't leave much ash, which is a testament to the fact that there are no additives.

I have a number of positive things to say about all-natural charcoal briquettes. They're portable, effective, relatively inexpensive, and reliable. Serious grill cooks, such as those who compete in Steak Cookoff Association events, pretty much always

use briquettes because they know exactly how much heat they'll be getting. They will actually measure out the precise number of briquettes into a chimney because they've pretty much calibrated the amount of heat that will be produced after a certain amount of time. (And most of them cook on PKs.)

While lump charcoal has often been prized as the more "natural" alternative to briquettes, now that we have all-natural briquettes, the differences between the two are fewer. Lump charcoal is, as it sounds, pieces of wood that have been carbonized whole, rather than broken down into dust and fine particles and then reassembled into briquettes. It has also been touted as contributing more flavor and burning hotter than briquettes, but I'm not sure about that either.

As any of you who regularly buy lump charcoal know, you are never sure what you're going to get in a bag. Sometimes it might be full of appealing chunks that resemble the pieces of wood they were before carbonization. Of course, the size is never consistent. Sometimes you'll have a ton of small shards, and other times you'll find pieces of former tree branches or roots that don't even fit in the chimney. Often, you'll find pieces of molding or joining wood that are clearly remnants from a furniture factory or some other production facility. In theory, this is a good thing, as we hope no useful wood goes to waste. But in practice, I'm a little skeptical that all the wood that goes into lump charcoal was carbonized in a raw, untreated state—and I certainly don't want chemicals in my charcoal. Furthering my doubt is the fact that I've found nails, pieces of wire, and other non-wood detritus in bags, suggesting that the producers aren't too strict in their processing.

As to whether lump charcoal offers more wood flavor, that's possible. You know when you light a chimney full of lump charcoal and it enters that phase of sparking and spitting out little embers for three or four minutes? Well, that's proof of an incomplete carbonization process. Little particles of leftover wood are getting heated and then exploding out of the charcoal as the water vaporizes. The preservation of some of the wood in the charcoal might provide a little woodsmoke character, but it's not bound to be much and is certainly no substitute for real wood.

Does it burn hotter? I've not found that to be the case, but it's hard to tell because of the randomness of the size and shape of lump charcoal pieces. If you filled one chimney full of briquettes and another full of lump charcoal, chances are the one full of briquettes would weigh more since they are uniform in shape and fill up the chimney more efficiently. More fuel weight means a more intense burn and a higher temperature.

Binchōtan

It's worth mentioning a special kind of charcoal from Japan (now also made in other countries) because it's pretty darn cool. Expensive but cool. This is the stuff you'd use to make yakitori in a konro grill—one of those narrow, boxlike tabletop grills meant for roasting skewers—because it burns hot and exceedingly clean with almost no smoke. It's the purest form of charcoal you can buy.

The skill of making binchōtan is a highly respected craft in Japan. It involves harvesting high-grade ubame oak—which is especially hard and has a fine grain—by hand from the particularly rugged forest terrain in which it grows. The wood is cut into long stalks taller than the average person, bundled, and then put into large kilns, in which a fire is built before the doors are sealed up with bricks and wet clay. An opening is left for air to enter, and there's an exhaust where steam and other vapors can escape. The total process takes about ten days, but what comes out are magical sticks comprising about 95 percent pure carbon (compared to the 50 to 70 percent you find in standard charcoal). When you tap two pieces together, they clang more like metal than wood.

Because of its purity, binchōtan is not as easy to light as standard charcoal. You can still place it in a chimney, but it might require a couple of refills of paper before it catches. Many people place their filled chimney over the flame of a gas burner for a few minutes to get it started. Even then, after it has caught, it still takes between twenty and forty minutes before it's glowing and fully heated.

Contrary to popular belief, binchōtan doesn't necessarily burn hotter than standard charcoal, but it definitely burns longer, often lasting for up to five hours and keeping a consistent temperature throughout. (Standard charcoal decreases in size and turns to ash in about thirty minutes.) If you're not going to use binchōtan for five hours—say, you don't own an izakaya—you can also submerge it in a bucket of water to cool it off. After it has cooled and dried, it can be used again just as effectively.

4
—

THE WHOLE FIRE
Coals, Flames, and Smoke

No matter how experienced you are in the kitchen, when cooking with wood, your most important job is to manage that fire. This is true whether you're maintaining a blaze in the firebox of an offset cooker or sustaining a coal bed on a grill to get just a flicker of smoke as you quickly cook some steaks. It takes a long time to get comfortable cooking with fire. Of course, cooking outdoors is appealing, except when it isn't—cold nights, hot nights, wet nights, late nights, snowy nights. But to gain meaningful experience, you have to do it regularly for a long time, as I did when we had our barbecue trailer and the restaurant. This means you will often be covered in grime and smell like smoke.

In a way, to cook with fire is to tend to its needs, to serve its interests so it will serve yours. After a while, live-fire cooking can get exhausting—even just a week or three, like when testing the recipes for this book. If you think about it, what makes modern cooking *modern* is the fact that you no longer have the burden of tightly managing your heat source. This has been true in every leap of cooking innovation, from the gas range to the electric stove to the microwave to sous vide. The evolution of cooking is about eliminating guesswork and removing some of the requirements of experience, feel, and intuition.

I've certainly made my share of mistakes in tending fires. I've used the wrong kind of wood, not enough of it, and too much of it. I've turned my back at the wrong time or missed the window when the coals are at their peak. There's always something to learn from these simple and universal errors.

This chapter is all about what I've learned from many years of staring into fires. I talk about essential tools, the stages of a fire, and the concept of using the *whole fire*: cooking different ingredients over the entire duration of a fire (from ignition to ash) to create a meal. Getting the most out of a fire (your principal ingredient) is not only efficient but also the greatest honor you can pay it.

I talk about lighting and maintaining the different kinds of fire you need for the various types of fire-related cooking in this book. The variability of fire makes recipes a little difficult to write, as your food may take more or less time to cook depending on the heat you generate.

And finally, I talk about smoke—how to attract it, collect it, and ultimately get the most out of it. Since it is the most important seasoning and a cooking method, taking smoke seriously is a hugely important aspect of the job.

THE STAGES OF FIRE

From the second a fire is lit to the moment it has truly gone out, you can chart its progression through separate but connected stages. Officially, the four stages of fire are ignition, growth, fully developed, and decay. (Too bad they couldn't find a single word for "fully developed"; it would sound a lot better.) But for the purposes of cooking, I look a little more granularly at fire, adding a couple more stages and using some slightly different terminology. My six stages of fire are ignition, white smoke, flame, coals, embers, and ash.

Understanding the stages of fire is important to cooking with the whole fire. Each embodies a unique dynamic of heat, flame, and smoke that can help you achieve nuanced and distinctive results in your cooking. In a fully blazing fire, all the stages are happening at the same time, which amounts to a chain reaction. (For this reason, some people consider the reaction itself to be another side of the fire triangle—fuel, heat, oxygen—and now call it the fire tetrahedron.) This chemical chain reaction occurs when each element acts on and enables the others, continuing the series of reactions without any additional external inputs. So, for instance, in a charcoal

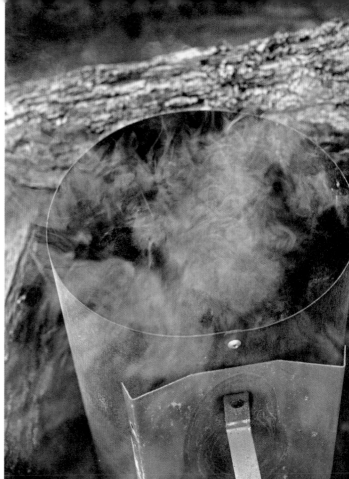

chimney, the heat generated by the burning of fuel contributes to the ignition of new fuel, or the departure of volatile gases draws in the oxygen to feed the fire.

IGNITION This is when the fire is just getting going. Or when, say, you've just lit the newspaper in a chimney to get the charcoal going. Be sure you have ample tinder with plenty of oxygen around it that is easily accessed by your spark.

WHITE SMOKE This stage, characterized by dehydration, begins after the wood or charcoal is ignited and heating but before it's fully burning. You'll recognize it by the billowing white smoke and steam—a mixture of water vapor, carbon dioxide, and volatile compounds. The water in the wood is literally boiling off, often leading to intense popping and the violent ejection of particles and sparks. As moisture dissipates, the fuel continues to warm.

FLAME Eventually, fire breaks out. You will see active and vigorous flames emanating from the wood. You may also have an intuitive sense of when the fire is thriving: there's a sound, a rhythm, a quickening to the noises it makes. It has a life of its own as it increases in heat, builds momentum. The smell of clean, sweet smoke starts to

surround the fire. An aura of heat beckons us in (but not too close!). Make sure the fire has plenty of available fuel at this time because it's also stabilizing itself, producing the foundation of heat it needs to continue the chain reaction. The smoke, you'll notice, will no longer billow gray and white; it becomes more transparent, maybe with a light gray to blue tint. This is the ideal time for indirect cooking. You can cook over the flames also, but not too closely or intensely. Without focused attention, it's far too easy to burn things at this stage unless the distance is such that the tips of the flames only occasionally lick the food.

COALS For those who are cooking or even just seeking warmth, this is the sweet part of the fire, its lifeblood. The wood has lost its water and burned down into its constituent elements, which are slowly being disassembled by the heat and chemical reactions of the fire. These constituent parts, made of the carbon and hydrocarbons (lignin, hemicellulose, and cellulose) at the heart of wood, glow and radiate intense heat, but the volatile gases that create flames have for the most part burned off. This is the coal bed.

At this point, many chefs will rake off some coals to cook over, while leaving the rest as the heat source onto which they'll periodically throw fresh logs to keep it going. The consistent, dry, and intense flameless heat from the coals enables searing, caramelization, and smoking.

EMBERS If you don't refuel the fire, the coals will eventually begin to peter out. They'll develop a thin coating of ash and some white smoke may return. The ash slows the passive intrusion of oxygen, further dampening the fire. If you want to revive it, add some light fuel, blow to clear off the ash, and fan the flames or continue to blow. This environment offers some nice opportunities for gentle cooking.

ASH The fire is dead. No amount of oxygen or fuel will rekindle it without significant heat. Funny enough, this stage is harder to achieve than you might think, which is why forest fires get started when campers think they've extinguished their campfire. (To be clear, when this happens, the campfire was in the embers stage when it should have been cinders/ash.) Once you've combed through the ashes and cinders and found no pockets of residual heat, feel free to rake up the remains and deposit them in your ash bucket. Larger chunks can be reused in your next fire. Just add them after the fire is going or relight in the chimney.

COOKING WITH THE WHOLE FIRE

There's no reason to waste a good fire. Making fires at home is not something most of us do every day, so it's good to make the most of it when you have it. That's why I love using the whole fire when I cook, that is, from the earliest, spiking moments past ignition and white smoke all the way to the slow, smoldering coals.

What might this look like?

> Before you dump the coals, blister vegetables over a red-hot chimney, which focuses and concentrates the heat.

> Put a wok over the chimney and stir-fry on it!

> Then, if you're still on charcoal, grill.

> Or close the lid of your cooker and roast or smoke something (say, a chicken) with a two-zone setup.

> Add wood to a firepit and cook over it directly. Cook steaks or chops quickly over the flames while cooking a large roast off the coals.

> Finally, slow roast vegetables, like onions, squashes, or eggplants, in the coals and embers.

Consider the whole, malleable life of a fire when planning a meal. Even if you're not camping or out in the woods, think like you are. How would you prepare a meal if the fire was your only heat source? How would you efficiently combine searing, blackening, roasting, smoking, and grilling to get the most out of one blaze?

By the way, meals in which every single item comes off the fire can be rather intense. After all, smoke is an incredibly powerful flavor. So keep each meal balanced and remember that you can grill or smoke ingredients not only for the next meal but also for meals later in the week.

ESSENTIAL FIRE TOOLS

You don't need a lot of equipment to handle a fire, but in the interests of safety, cleanliness, and workflow, these are the tools I keep on hand.

ASH BUCKET Cleaning out ash is the unfortunate penance we all pay for the joys of outdoor cooking. Having a dedicated receptacle makes the job much easier. A simple galvanized bucket or can is easy to find at a hardware store. Ash is very heavy and dense, so look for one that's big enough to suit your cooker or firepit but not so big that you can't lift it. Also, make sure the bucket has a lid to keep the rain out so the bottom doesn't rust out. Let fresh ash sit in the bucket for at least a number of days before disposing, as you never know what's still smolder-ing. Down here in Texas, it's so hot that it may take more than a week for all of the coals to die out—and you don't want to start a dumpster fire.

CHIMNEY If you don't already use a chimney to light your charcoal, I don't know what to say. It's the easiest, cleanest, and most efficient way to start a cook. If you're going for a real outdoor-kitchen setup with a smoker, a grill, and even a firepit or side fire, I suggest that you invest in two chimneys because sometimes you need to get a second one started while the first one is already going. (Tip: To start a second chimney, put it right on top of the lit grill or even the first lit chimney.) Also, I recommend buying large chimneys. You'll find a number of smaller chimneys on hardware store shelves, but nothing's more annoying than not being able to spark up as much charcoal as you need. And if you need less than a large one holds, just fill it up halfway! Weber still makes the stan-dard go-to chimney. It can get beat up pretty fast and doesn't always last more than a year, but it works well enough.

CLOSED-TOE SHOES You'll never see me in a pair of flip-flops or sandals around a fire, even in the summer, even if I'm playing the lead in a staging of *Julius Caesar*. (Won't catch me in a toga either!) I know plenty of people who exclusively sport sandals when the weather heats up. But hear me, friends, you want to wear closed-toe shoes during a cook. Ever try dumping a chimney full of hot coals with bare feet? Don't do it. Be safe and injury-free. Let's keep those toesies unburned!

FIREBRICKS These heavy fireproof bricks are useful to have around and can be deployed and redeployed depending on your needs. Put them on top of your grill grates and rest another grilling surface on top of the bricks to crudely mimic the action of a Santa Maria grill (see page 45). Stack them like LEGOs to build a makeshift konro grill for searing yakitori skewers. Lay them flat as a platform on which to set your charcoal chimney after dumping. So many uses! The only downside is their weight.

FIRE TONGS This is my preferred tool for finely manipulating logs in a firepit or firebox. I use extra long ones to reach into fireboxes and firepits from a safe distance. I often shift and rearrange the structure of my fires, and tongs are never far from my hand.

HOSE WITH A SPRAYER Hey, summer is hot and dry and only getting hotter and drier in many places. So I always keep a hose with a powerful nozzle nearby and set to on, just in case I need to hose something down quickly or to spritz the ground around my cooker before I go night-night.

SHOVEL A good old-fashioned shovel has been my number-one tool for as long as I've been cooking barbecue. Its uses are almost countless, but you'll mainly want one for manipulating and shaping your fire in the firebox. For a large, professional cooker like we use at the restaurant, any heavy-duty shovel will do. For a firebox the size of the one in the Franklin Pit, I recommend something

smaller. You want a forty-eight-inch-long handle so you can reach all the way to the back of the firebox without having to stick your hands too close to the fire. Shovels are also essential for firepit cooking, which involves lots of shifting around of logs and coals. And if you've got a side fire going, you'll want a full-size shovel for transporting a load of coals from it to your cooker.

TROWEL I don't use one, but Jordan swears by this handy mini-shovel, particularly when configuring coals in a PK or kettle grill or even shifting things around in a Big Green Egg. They're inexpensive and come in different shapes and sizes. He recommends keeping a few around. And when you're not using them for cooking, they're great for repotting petunias.

BUILDING FIRE

I used to be kind of orthodox about only lighting a fire with wood and a little piece of butcher paper dabbed with brisket fat or cooking oil. But I have to admit that, in my old age, I've softened a bit. Nowadays, I might start by lighting a few charcoal briquettes and letting them start the wood. And there's no getting around the fact that there are all kinds of idiot-proof thingamajigs available to help, like those little hockey pucks you light with a match that keep burning until your charcoal or kindling gets going. (Even I use those things when they're around, so yeah, definitely idiot-proof.)

However, I still use the log-cabin method to stack my logs in a square on top of one another, two or three logs high, depending on the size of the fire I'm building. (Two heavy logs on the bottom, lighter ones in the middle, and a heavy one on top; so, when the middle logs collapse, the heavy one drops in.) If I'm making a fire inside the small firebox of the Franklin Pit, I'll stack up about six mini-logs and drop in some hot charcoal. If I'm building a bigger fire in the firepit, I'll make the same structure but use full-size logs.

To create fire you need three things: fuel, heat, and oxygen. That's called the "fire triangle" because you can't have a fire without all three elements. The log cabin is an elegant and simple structure that ensures each of the three elements is present. The wood is obviously the fuel. In the middle of the log cabin's square, you place a little extra fuel—some kindling and tinder in the form of newspaper, wood shavings, or charcoal. The loose openings between the stacked logs allow oxygen to easily access the tinder and continue to supply the growing reaction.

Many people confuse fire for heat but, the fact is, fire is an ongoing chemical reaction whose effects we perceive as light and heat. If you want to put out a fire, remove one of the three elements (hence the lid on the ash can). Heat is introduced at the beginning in the form of a match, a lighter, or one of those thingamajigs, which is placed in the middle next to the tinder. (In the firepit, I often just light some charcoal in a chimney and either dump it into the middle of the log cabin or build the log cabin around my chimney and remove the chimney once the logs catch.) That should do the trick. Just wait a while and you'll have fire.

The triangle is important because if you're having trouble keeping your fire going, you know how to diagnose the problem. Are you lacking fuel, oxygen, or heat? The latter is the one element that many people have trouble with yet don't realize. If you overload your fire with fuel but don't have enough heat to cause the chemical reaction, you won't have fire. Also, remember that a log of firewood on its own isn't solely fuel. If it's green (carrying a lot of water), it contains a ton of anti-fuel, which makes it hard to generate enough heat. The temperature of your fuel has an impact too. Really cold wood takes longer to light (and removes energy from an already-lit fire). While I don't generally feel the need to pre-warm logs inside the firebox, in cold weather I will occasionally place a piece or two of wood on top of the firebox or on the perimeter of the firepit—especially if they're somewhat green—just so they are rarin' and ready to go when I throw them on.

CONTROLLING FIRE

You want to be the boss of your fire, not the other way around. Being in total control is a major requirement for successful cooking. It's very easy to let a fire get away from you in one way or another and end up cooking over insufficient heat or too much heat or with bad smoke. If this doesn't ruin your expensive ingredients, it will at least make them far less delicious than they should be and can be super-frustrating.

Luckily, you can control fire with surprising accuracy if you carefully consider what you're doing and *plan ahead*. That is, many of the adjustments you can make to a fire don't have instant results—they may take some time to develop. To stay on top of your game, you need to think a couple of moves ahead. What does this look like? Your approach isn't too different whether you're tending an offset cooker, a kamado, a live fire in a firepit, or coals in a grill.

If you need to lower the temperature in an offset cooker, close the firebox door a smidge (but never too much) to restrict airflow. Use your shovel to slide the coal bed back toward the firebox door, where it will leak some heat out the back side; this makes the heat less aggressive. If you need to raise the temperature quickly, push the coal bed forward toward the cook chamber or add a quick-burning piece of well-seasoned wood. If you need to bring the heat up over twenty minutes or so, add a larger piece of denser wood that will take a little while to get going but anchor the fire for another half hour or so.

Lowering the temperature in a Big Green Egg or kamado grill is one of the challenges of these cookers. But you can always close the vents a bit to minimize oxygen intake or open the lid periodically to let excess heat out until the whole thing dies down.

When tending an open fire in a firepit, the shovel is always your friend. I constantly shift logs and coals around depending on the needs of what I'm cooking. Pay attention to the direction of the breeze and expose your fire to it if you want a burst of heat. Conversely, shield the fire against the sides of the firepit if you want less flame. Throw on heavy wood to dampen a fire for a while (and have a place to move it off if you don't want a deluge of flame and heat).

To drop the intensity of the radiant heat on a grill, use tongs or a trowel to spread out the coals.

You got this—after all, you're just one more person following along after thirty-eight thousand years of people cooking over flames. Fire may seem intimidating, but if you have the right tools and ample space, you will be the one in control.

SIDE FIRES AND BURN BARRELS

One thing that you always need on a cook is a backup supply of fresh coals. That could be in the form of a chimney full of charcoal, lit and ready to go. But in the event you want to cook over only wood coals—my favorite way, but not always the most practical—you need a second supply of wood that's ready to go. One of the advantages of firepit cooking—especially if your firepit is big enough—is that you can always separate fresh coals from the larger fire and cook over them directly. But if you're cooking on a PK or kettle grill and you want fresh wood coals, the answer is a side fire.

One good reason to keep an old grill or firepit around, even if you don't use it much, is as a place to burn down a couple of logs so you're fully stocked with fresh wood coals as you need them. Then you can just shovel or bucket them over to your grill in the exact quantity needed for what you're cooking. Also, in cooler weather, it's a nice way to keep yourself warm!

Another alternative is what is commonly used in whole hog cooking: the burn barrel. This contraption is usually made from an old steel drum and a few pieces of rebar that have been driven through a foot or so above the bottom of the drum to create a matrix whose openings are not quite large enough to let a log fall through. A good-size opening—big enough to get a shovel in—is cut in the bottom of the barrel. After igniting a bunch of logs in the barrel, the fire quickly burns the wood and drops the coals down onto the ground (firebricks or another inflammable surface).

These can then be shoveled off and used. Keep adding wood as needed. In fact, this is a good place to use fairly green wood, as these barrels create a serious inferno (keep them away from anything burnable). It's the exact same principle often seen with wood grills at restaurants, where logs are stacked in a cage at the rear of the grill. The bottom logs on fire slowly drop their coals down to the surface, and the grill chef rakes them into use.

TIPS FOR SUCCESSFUL FIRE COOKS

These tips will help you manage your fire effortlessly so you can keep your attention focused on what you're cooking.

Set yourself up for success.

French chefs call it mise en place, roughly, "everything in its place." What it means, basically, is to be physically prepared. Have all of your tools ready and within easy reach. Think through your systems. Do you have a handy place to dump waste? If you need water, do you have access to it? How many different knives will you need and are they all within easy reach? With fire cooking, this means having all the firewood you need at the ready. It means having tongs, spray bottles, sheet pans, and towels at hand for when you need them.

Preheat, preheat.

Cooking on an apparatus that's not fully at the desired temperature is a surefire way to slow things down or cook poorly. For that reason, give your cooker or grill time to heat up, which often means starting earlier than dinnertime. Get your cooker going and allow it not only to reach the right temperature but to hold it for a good ten or fifteen minutes. This prep will make the rest of your cook so much better.

Patience pays off.

Along with the principle of preheating, having the patience to let your fire get to the proper stage is key. How many times have you dumped your chimney of charcoal too soon? You put your food on the grill and the temperature is *waaaay* too hot, so your food cooks too quickly and unevenly or flares up and burns. With all forms of fire, patience pays. Give yourself enough time to be sure the coal bed is at the right heat, it's not spiking too much, and it will last as long as you need it to.

Have backup ready.

Have the additional coals you may need at the ready to keep your fire controlled. Say you're cooking chicken pieces on the bone, and they're going to take longer than one chimney of charcoal is going to give you. Well, have a second chimney going for the moment you predict that to happen. I've had second chimneys going that I just allowed to burn out because didn't end up needing the coals. Yes, the charcoal was wasted, but better that than not having enough heat to finish the cook.

COOKING WITH SMOKE

Smoke, the inspiration for this book and one of the foundations of everything I've done professionally, is something with which I have a rather complex relationship these days. Perhaps because I've been around it almost continuously for many years now, I approach smoke with more apprehension than when I was just a bright-eyed fledgling looking to get that enticing smoky flavor onto brisket. These days, as my knowledge of smoke has grown, my approach has become quite a bit more nuanced, as has my taste for it.

Without question, smoke remains an alluring flavor for many people. However, it's also important to consider whether you're using good smoke or bad smoke and enough smoke or too much smoke. While the title of this book may suggest a full-throated endorsement of smoke culture, it's not that simple. I support a subtle, measured approach to smoke and want to talk about how to get good flavor and in just the right amount. I see smoke as a seasoning, and just as with any seasoning—salt, hot sauce, cilantro (yuck!)—moderation is key.

What Is Smoke?

A remarkable substance, smoke is a staggeringly complex mixture of gases, liquids, and solid particles that can range from visible specks of ash to microscopic molecules. The incomplete combustion of wood results in smoke, and the temperature of the fire dictates which particles are released and at what time. As wood is broken down during combustion, these components interact with ingredients in complex ways.

Research has shown that the visible part of smoke has the least (positive) impact on food. The vaporous or gaseous elements (invisible to the naked eye) are the most influential and desirable. The color of the resulting smoke can actually tell you something about its qualities. The hotter the fire, the smaller the particles. So if the wood went through complete combustion—requiring extraordinarily high temperatures—the by-products would be mostly carbon dioxide and water as well as some ash. Its "smoke" would be clear, as the particulate matter would be invisibly fine.

Poor combustion happens when there's not enough heat or oxygen and results in a large amount of very heavy particles, like tar and creosote—gross stuff. Those heavy particles absorb light and look sooty—black and gray in a viscerally unappealing way.

COLD SMOKING VERSUS HOT SMOKING

Primarily a method of food preservation, cold smoking can certainly be practiced at home, but you'll need both your smoke chamber to be far enough from the heat so the food doesn't cook and some sort of mechanism or setup that helps the airflow. Some methods of cold smoking suggest using the smoke from a cool or barely smoldering combustion, which, as you know, I think yields an undesirably dirty smoke.

Cold smoking is also tricky. It requires its ingredients to sit from several hours to several days at room temperature or slightly warmer. Furthermore, the low-acid environment of meat and the absence of oxygen create a dangerous breeding ground for bacteria, especially the spores that cause botulism. Because of this, cold-smoked meats are cured with sodium nitrate, which itself needs to be used with care. Long story short, if errors are made in temperature control, precise dosing of salt and preservatives, and other forms of food safety and storage, much can go wrong.

Hot smoking is much easier and requires no special equipment. It's as forgiving as it is delicious, and as long as you cook your meat to the proper internal temperature, you don't have to worry about getting sick. Unless you're really serious about cold smoking from a technical point of view, it's probably best left to the experts while you fire up your coals for a classic hot smoke.

White smoke is a little better, but smoke that looks faintly blue is the result of just the right amount of incomplete combustion. The fire is hot enough to break down the wood to finer particles that reflect the blue spectrum. This is the smoke that has the best flavor and the most nuanced impact on your food. It is created when your fire is between 600° and 750°F, which is where we aim to keep ours at the restaurant. It is also why I love the offset smoker, which supports the high temperatures that create such fine smoke in a moderate-size cooking space.

Carbonyls, which are released at lower temperatures when the wood compounds of cellulose and hemicellulose are being dismantled, primarily contribute to the browning of meat. At this stage, gasified acetic and formic acids add subtle hints of citric tartness and bitterness. At higher temperatures (around 600°F), lignin starts to break down, releasing phenols into the smoke. The phenols are what carry most of the flavors that we associate with smoke, both good (savory, smoky spice) and bad (medicinal and bitter).

One phenol, syringol, has the textbook flavor of smoke, while guaiacol (also present in oak wine barrels) offers toasty and spice notes, and vanillin imparts creamy sweetness. Phenols also have antimicrobial effects that sanitize meat, allowing it to be preserved for prolonged periods, yet another solid reason why you want to smoke with high combustion and aim for that fine blue smoke.

Attracting Smoke

Once you have your fire burning nice and hot and clean blue smoke is emanating from the stack, the next goal is to get your food in the best possible position to accumulate smoke. Although it seems like smoke gets into everything it touches, it actually just gets onto ingredients. Penetration doesn't reach very deep into the food, which is a good thing if you don't want too much smoke. Your taste buds do the work of merging the smoky flavor of the meat's exterior with the moist, meaty flavor of the interior.

Given that, it's important to attract plenty of smoke onto the outside of the meat. However, even in the very smoky environment of an offset cooker, smoke doesn't want to settle on the surface of the meat because of a very thin veneer of static air that surrounds objects. Known as the boundary layer, this is a concept most frequently used in the physics of turbulence (as with airplane wings). In our case, the boundary layer repulses smoke from the meat's surface.

To attract smoke, you want to keep the meat's exterior moist. Smoke particles move from warm to cool surfaces, and the constant evaporation that occurs on the surface of moist meat keeps it cooler than the surrounding air (even in the oven-like heat of a smoker), attracting the particles in smoke. Moisture also helps to trap the smoke particles when they do contact the meat. This is one reason why I periodically spray the exterior of the meat during a cook. (But be careful with that spray bottle. Excess wetting can remove smoke! The surface just needs to be a little damp.)

Finally, rubs also help, as the uneven surfaces they create flummox the boundary layer and attract smoke particles.

Delivering Smoke

Given the range of smoke's characteristics, it's important to get elements of each into the mix. Luckily, the chain reaction of the fire means that, to some degree, all of the qualities of smoke are available simultaneously: new wood starts to burn as old coals are exhausted. One of the benefits of having a strong fire and coal bed is that the smoky by-products of lower-temperature burning are minimized because newly introduced wood spends a much shorter time in that state before its lignin starts offering up those tasty phenols.

Still, it takes a good long while for smoke to accumulate enough phenols to get that complex, even, and tasteful flavor. Can you have too much smoke? In a word, yes! Every piece of food has its own smoke threshold, meaning the amount of smoke that tastes good on it. Something like a brisket, rich in gelatin and fat, can take a lot of smoke. But a chicken wants far less—just enough to add savory complexity to each bite.

Typically, you get a sense for how much smoke naturally wants to accrue by observing the surface of the meat. As the surface dries, it will stop attracting as much smoke. If you want more smoke, keep spraying and wetting the meat. At some point, however, this becomes a futile proposition, as the pellicle (a thin coating of proteins on the surface of the meat) will evaporate faster than you can keep it wet. By then you can be sure your food is plenty smoky, but I don't recommend even getting to that stage. Once you've reached a desired texture or color, you've probably gone far enough.

Throw too much smoke or stale smoke when there's not much airflow and you'll have something nasty and bitter. If you have a good temperature but not enough smoke—such as when your heat comes from charcoal but not enough wood—you'll just end up with roast beef. But when slow and steady wins the day, you'll have the perfect accretion that is the definition of good smoke.

REPELLING SMOKE—AVERT YOUR EYES!

While smoke is an appealing ingredient to our taste buds, it's not so appealing to the rest of our body, which is why it's important to get in the habit of only taking in the most minimal, unavoidable amount of smoke while cooking with fire. The number-one practice that I observe every time I open the smoker door is turning my head, closing my eyes, and holding my breath. Once it's been open for a second and the initial wave of smoke has rushed by me, I turn my head back and open my eyes to check out the meat, then maybe hit it with the spray bottle, all while holding my breath. After three to five seconds total, I close the smoker door and breathe sweet, fresh air!

5
—

WARMING UP

Essential Pantry Items, Tools, and Rubs, Spices, and Sauces

Preparation is the foundation of good cooking and is especially important when working with fire and smoke. While the term *prep* applies to being well equipped with regard to tools and materials, it also refers to creating a schedule, getting your mind straight, and building flavor through process. When a meal is going to take upward of twelve hours to cook, you need to have a fair idea of the plot points ahead of time, especially if you've got a hungry family to feed or guests to serve. It may sound like a drag to sit down and sketch out in a notebook the timeline of a brisket cook, but you want to know that your food is going to be ready at the time it's needed—and when barbecuing at home, that's not always easy to accomplish.

Most of the dishes in this book call for dry brines, marination, air-drying, fermentations, tempering, and the like. These are all simple methods that can be done hours or days ahead, making the day of your dinner quicker and easier. Just because these crucial processes happen well in advance, they shouldn't be ignored or minimized. And just a tiny bit of early work can drastically improve the flavor and texture of your food and the way it cooks.

CREATING A COOKING TIMELINE

Whether I'm doing a short cook or a long one, I always plot a timeline to keep me on schedule. It is a form of temporal mise en place in which I outline a timed sequence of events from the beginning of a dish to the end, inclusive of everything from shopping and prepping to lighting fires and warming cookers to carryover cooking and resting. A timeline is a road map *and* an insurance plan if something gets off schedule or I get tired and mentally fuzzy. It allows me to trace back along my path to determine what I have or haven't done. When you start a cook on one day and finish it on another (or start so early in the morning that it feels like a different day by the time you serve the food), you'll be happy to have a written plan guiding you.

Since serving the food is what it's all about, that's where you start writing your timeline. Just as any restaurant kitchen has prep sheets for its cooks, you will fully plan out your menu and write down all the steps to cooking it, including making a list of the plates, platters, and tongs you need as well as all the ingredients for the cook. These are the puzzle pieces that must be assembled correctly for everything to go off without a hitch. For instance, if you're planning a brisket cook, you would ask yourself the following questions: How long will it take to cook that brisket? How long to trim it? At what time do I hope to wrap? How long will the carryover be? If I get behind, where can I make up time?

Begin with the moment you want to eat and work your way backward. So if you want to sit down to brisket with friends at 6:00 p.m., you might factor a two-hour rest (depending on conditions) starting at 4:00 p.m. That brisket would come off the cooker at 4:00 p.m., perhaps after a three-hour cooking window following wrapping. That means you'll wrap in the 1:00 p.m. range. Wrapping is often performed eight to nine hours after putting the brisket on. So, working back from 1:00 p.m., this means the brisket needs to be on the smoker at 4:00 a.m., which means you need to be up and firing up your smoker by 3:00 a.m. And that means trimming and rubbing it at 3:00 a.m., although I almost always trim it the night before and pull it out of the fridge to temper and rub when I get up. You should also probably factor an additional hour somewhere along the line as a safety net. For some extra guidance, I might jot down the projected temperatures that I want to hit at key points along the way, just as I watch for mile markers on a road trip.

In the end, your timeline will look something like this:

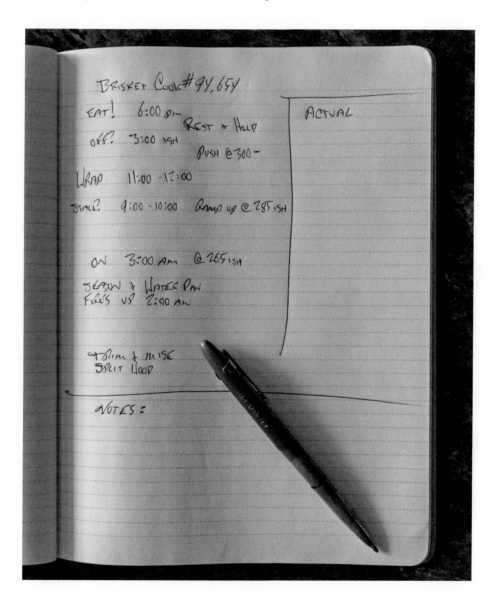

Doing a timeline for every dish—or, at least, every major one—may seem like an absurd amount of organization but, trust me, it really helps. If you get into the habit of doing this, you won't end up like Jordan, who often admits he should have lit the coals earlier as he and his wife, Christie, and their dinner guests sit down to dine at 9:30 p.m.

ESSENTIAL PANTRY ITEMS

To shore up your prep and prevent unexpected, time-consuming hiccups, like having to run to the store for more salt or oil, keep your pantry well and simply stocked. I don't use much in the way of spices or herbs. I like the flavor of the food to merge with the flavor of the fire—and leave it at that. As a result, my pantry is exceedingly basic, made up mostly of oils, vinegars, salts, lemons, garlic, fermented goods, and some spices. Here are my go-to items.

APPLE CIDER AND OTHER VINEGARS Apple cider vinegar is so central to my process that I buy it by the jug and keep a spray bottle of it on hand, whether I'm cooking in the smoker, on the firepit, or on the grill.

That said, I love the flavors of many different vinegars, so I keep red wine and white wine versions around, as well as sherry, balsamic, and especially rice.

BLACK PEPPER I use pre-ground 16-mesh (coarse) black pepper in our rubs and also keep a grinder handy (the incredible Männkitchen Pepper Cannon) for freshly ground black pepper.

CITRUS Acidity is key to making your dishes pop, so be sure your citrus bowl is always stocked with fresh lemons, oranges, and limes. I use the zest and peel of citrus in lots of dishes and preps. But, of course, the juice is also crucial. After you remove the zest from a citrus fruit, wrap up the fruit and keep it in the fridge so you can also use the juice later.

FERMENTED FOODS Sauerkraut, kimchi, and other naturally fermented foods are a constant around the house, as these condiments add instant complexity and contrast to whatever's coming off the fire.

GARLIC A miraculous little seasoning, fresh garlic not only can last unrefrigerated for weeks at a time (making it convenient to store) but it packs a huge punch, so use it in moderation. Yes, peeling garlic can be a chore, but pre-peeled cloves never have as much flavor as what you break off a whole head. If using it uncooked, tempering freshly minced garlic in vinegar or citrus juice for 10 to 15 minutes takes the edge off.

GRAPESEED OIL This is my oil of choice for most cooking needs because it has a high smoke point (good for cooking at very high temperatures) and neutral flavor. I keep it in restaurant-style squeeze bottles for mess-free delivery.

HOT SAUCE I love to make my own hot sauce, but I also keep bottles of other sauces around. Forever on my shelf are Crystal Hot Sauce and Yellowbird Jalapeño sauce (a delicious local product). I like these not just for the spice but also the acidity.

PICKLED ITEMS Continuing on the theme of acidity, it goes without saying that pickles of all shapes, sizes, and kinds play a huge role in my diet and in my pantry. They are great for garnishes, side dishes, condiments, and snacks.

SALT Kosher is my go-to cooking salt. The granule size and coarseness make it easy to handle when pinching and dusting and keep me from oversalting. Morton Coarse Kosher Salt is denser than Diamond Crystal Kosher Salt, so be sure you're calibrated to whichever one you're using.

For finishing salt, I use something along the lines of Maldon Sea Salt Flakes or Jacobsen Salt Co. Pure Flake Sea Salt. These are both beautiful, crunchy, mineral flakes that look and taste delicious, offering pleasant minerality and a soft, not-too-sharp flavor.

SPICES I don't keep a ton of spices around, but they tend to include chile powders, paprika, and other savory items that deliver a little kick. These also would include rubs and seasonings such as Lawry's, which I mention on page 110.

COOKING TOOLS

I love kitchen gadgets—utensils, knives, pots, pans, thermometers, scales—everything. My ever-expanding collection of kitchen equipment is the bane of Stacy's existence (well, one of the banes, at least). My excuse is that as a restaurant owner, cook, recipe developer, and constant answerer of questions, I need to be informed. But believe me, I get it when Stacy exclaims, "Maybe we don't need forty sheet pans at home."

Confoundingly, and to her point, I also believe that you need very little stuff for cooking. Some pieces of equipment can make your life easier and your cooking a little more refined and accurate, but you can also work around a lot of these gadgets if you don't have the space or the money . . . or you *do* have a significant other who deplores (kitchen) clutter.

So please view the following information through two lenses: (1) the things you *need* and (2) the things you might *want*. I try to make clear which items I put in which camp. But some tools—like smokers and grills, tongs and grates—are simply nonnegotiable.

CAST-IRON/CARBON-STEEL PANS Having durable and heat-resistant pans that you can throw on a fire or the coals are essential for all kinds of fire cooking. Sometimes you want to use the heat and a bit of the smoke generated by your fire while enjoying the ease of cooking in a pan. Also, even if you're cooking on a fire, you don't want every item to taste of the fire. The open-flame grill pan with perforations by Made In is very versatile. You get the best of both worlds—a sear from the steel plus the kiss of the fire—and it keeps your ingredients from falling into the coals.

CHAIR If you prepped well, you won't be scrambling around the whole time you're cooking. After all, barbecuing is supposed to be relaxing and enjoyable. You'll want to find moments here and there to take a load off, rest those dogs, and enjoy the outdoors while contemplating the weather, reading a magazine, or just daydreaming. So make sure you have a comfy outdoor chair, plus a few extras for a friend or two to relax in—everyone wants to sit by a fire.

COLD DRINKS AND ICE CHEST Don't mind if I do. An ice chest full of cold beverages is essential to your cook, unless it's a frigid midwinter evening. But let's imagine that, most of the time, the conditions are peachy, and you'll want refreshment whether you are quick-searing steaks or nursing a brisket for the long haul. My only caution: apply moderation. Be wary of the sneaky drinks, such as high-ABV beers, like IPAs, and especially well-made cocktails that magically disappear in seconds. This approach is, to a large degree, how I became a lager or pilsner or light ale guy over time. I love a crisp and refreshing beverage that has just enough alcohol to ease the passing of time without me forgetting something, making mistakes, or falling asleep—all of which can easily happen when you're planning to be up a good part of the night cooking for the next day.

A good ice chest is a cold drink's bestie, of course. I've been using YETI brand since it first came on the market, and to my mind, no chest offers a better combination of form-factor, insulating power, and lightweight mobility. YETI chests are expensive, however, and the fact is, any cooler will do—even a cheapie that's not the best quality—as long as you keep it filled with fresh ice.

COOK'S NOTEBOOK Keeping a notebook to record timelines (see page 94), recipe ideas, shopping lists, and everything that goes into a significant cook is essential. I never used to date my entries, which I regret now. Sometimes I look back on twelve years of recipes and the details of when and how I developed a certain method feel really valuable. So, as always, don't lose track of time.

FISH SPATULA No other spatula is thin enough to slide under a delicate skin to unstick it from a hot pan or grill surface without mangling the fish. But this is also a hardy enough tool to wonderfully flip all kinds of foods besides fish.

FLASHLIGHT I've got decent outside lighting for my setup, but there are times during a late-night cook when shadows get in the way. Having a good flashlight handy is always wise.

HEADLAMP

I've never seen Aaron wear a headlamp, but my outdoor setup is not as refined, nor is my technique and timing as immaculate, and I often find myself finishing something in the dark that was meant to be done long before. For this reason, I find a headlamp to be invaluable. After a bit of shopping around, I chose the Nitecore NU25 for its brightness but especially for its wide field of illumination, which is helpful if you have a few things going on at the same time. —Jordan

FOIL Surely you already keep a good supply of aluminum foil around your house. I get the industrial-size rolls from a restaurant supply store. All the standard household uses apply, but foil can also be fashioned into a durable, malleable, heat-conducting cooking vessel. There's no better way to get the most out of your fire than to turn a piece of foil into a boat for fish or into an envelope in which to seal vegetables and other ingredients to steam away in their own juices.

GRILL/FRYER BASKET Most grill baskets are small, weak, and overpriced. That's why I go to a restaurant-supply store and buy fryer baskets of all shapes and sizes. For vegetables and smaller items that might easily slip through the bars of the grate, a tight-mesh grill basket is a really handy thing. It's not expensive, but it also doesn't last too long, so don't worry if you have to replace it once a year or so.

(EXTRA) GRILL GRATES The idea that the sooty black crust that forms on the grill grate adds "flavor" or "soul" each time you cook on it is not only a myth but also positively detrimental to your cook. The only flavors a dirty grate might add to your ingredient are burnt and carbonized along with a sooty, ashy color. That said, a used grate is hard to clean. If you're entertaining or just tired after a long day, you might not get to washing your grate until the next day (or, let's be real, the next week or . . . never). While it's worthwhile to put a little elbow grease into keeping those things bright and shiny, it's also okay to replace them once they get beyond recuperation.

KITCHEN SCALE I'm a big believer in the accuracy, simplicity, and scalability of measuring ingredients by weight, not volume, so a good kitchen scale, like the Ohaus, is a high-priority item. After all, a cup of brown sugar will have varying weights depending on how tightly it's packed. It's really easy to build recipes such as sauces and rubs on a scale. Just put a bowl on the scale and tare it, which returns the reading to zero. Add your first ingredient, tare the scale again to return to zero, add the next ingredient, tare again, and so on. This is a beautifully simple and supremely accurate way to cook!

KNIVES While it's true that any old knife will do most of the time as long as its decently sharp, there are certain pleasures and advantages in being a bit of a knife geek, which I am. I simply find pleasure in owning and caring for an exquisite, handmade tool that's been carefully considered and crafted to have a certain balance, weight, and action. When you use such a knife, you can feel all of these qualities: the way it accurately, cleanly, and effortlessly slices and how it feels connected to your body so you don't get sore. A good knife makes prepping and serving a joy, not a chore—like a jazz drummer having the right drumstick.

I'm on record for liking a mass-produced, machine-made Dexter Russell serrated knife for slicing brisket, and I stand by that. It's excellent at getting through supertender, jiggly brisket while keeping the meat and bark intact (if you do it right). I also use that knife for all kinds of other tasks, such as breaking down prime rib.

There is much ado about Japanese versus Western knives, and I think both traditions offer incredible products. Japanese knives are typically thinner, made of harder steel, and have a single bevel (sharpened on only one side), which allows them to slice more cleanly. They are better for precision work and pure slicing, the most common techniques used in much of Japanese cooking. Western-style knives,

such as those made by Wüsthof or J. A. Henckels, are heavier, made of softer steel, and have two bevels (both sides are sharpened and come to a V-like point). This style is considered more versatile—it's a capable slicer, but it's also good for chopping, scraping, and crushing, which are more usual in Western cuisine. In a Western kitchen, it's common to have one or two all-purpose knives that can perform most tasks so you don't have to constantly switch blades. By contrast, Japanese cooks may constantly swap among a number of highly specialized tools.

Although you can find plenty of examples of pure styles, many manufacturers produce blades that blend or overlap the two traditions, such as Japanese-made Western chef's knives that apply the best of the Japanese craft to the Western double-beveled design. These hybrid knives are the kind that I use most often at home.

KNIFE SHARPENING

When my knives get a little dull, I sharpen them, and you should do the same. A sharp knife is a pleasing knife. When you have a high-quality blade, you need a quality sharpening protocol that takes sharpening shortcuts (like the inexpensive, little plastic tools) out of the equation.

First, you need a whetstone. While many sources say you a need a wide range of grits, I keep just one stone with 1,000 grit on one side and 5,000 grit on the other. I bought a rubber holder from Korin, a knife shop in New York with an online store, to secure the stone to the countertop. I often ignore the instruction to soak the stone in water for thirty to sixty minutes before using, because I usually don't know an hour ahead of time that I'm going to want to sharpen a knife. Instead, I keep a bowl of warm water handy and repeatedly splash water on the stone as I run the knives across it. It is important to hit the right angle as you rub the blade on the steel, a skill that takes practice and attention. Don't forget to press down hard enough that you actually grind the metal.

For the most part, I sharpen on the 5,000-grit side of the stone only. It's a fine grain that is perfectly good for honing and maintaining the edge of a knife that's been well cared for. Occasionally, I may take a few swipes on the 1,000 grit if a knife really needs some help, but that's rare because I keep my knives in good condition. If I want a superfine edge, I'll finish it on a piece of printer paper. Some people use a leather strop, but paper works just fine. Many chefs use a steel, though I never do. If you keep your blades sharp, you really don't need to.

SOME OF MY FAVORITE KNIFE MAKERS

CHUBO Founded by an American, this company is a retailer and producer that commissions craftspeople across Japan to create blades while also curating a diverse selection of quality Japanese knives. Its website is very informative about the various styles of Japanese blades.

MAC Much more affordable than Nenox and of amazing quality, MAC is a Japanese brand geared toward Western styles. However, the edge has a bit of a Japanese pitch to it, making it a more acute slicer than most Western-style blades.

MISONO This is another terrific and less-expensive Japanese knifemaker. These sturdy, classically shaped knives (many incorporate excellent Swedish steel) really hold their edge. The ten-inch chef's knife in carbon steel is Jordan's main blade.

NENOX These are my go-to knives. Nenox is a line of Western-style knives made by Nenohi in Japan. Unfortunately, they've become much more expensive than when I first bought them years ago—and they were expensive then. But they're amazing to work with. Their proprietary alloy of stainless steel is durable and keeps its edge but is soft enough to sharpen easily at home. The weight, balance, and feel of the knives are incredible. If you're awash in bitcoin money, consider these!

STEELPORT These are very cool, exceptionally crafted knives made from American materials in one of my favorite cities, Portland, Oregon. Founded in 2020, STEELPORT is a fairly new company. The knives are not discernably Western or Japanese in style. They combine elements of many knife-making traditions in original and highly functional tools.

MOP The word *mop* applies to both the tool and the mixture of ingredients that the tool adds to the food. In this case, I'm talking about the tool, which is a mini-version of what a janitor may wield while cleaning a floor. You could use a spoon for the purpose of applying a (ingredient) mop, but it tends to be less thorough. You can make your own mop from an old towel or other absorptive fabric, or you can buy a dedicated tool.

It's possible to use a standard kitchen brush to apply a mop, as long as you use the brush as a mop and not a brush. That is, don't let the brush (tool) touch the meat because you don't want to rub any sauce off or disturb the bark. So use a mop to apply a mop, but if you use a brush, never brush!

PEPPER GRINDER Black pepper and smoke were meant for each other. The crackling energy in black peppercorns echoes and intertwines with the snap and hiss of a live fire, so having a good pepper grinder is essential. For me, there is only one grinder to rule them all: the Männkitchen Pepper Cannon. Rarely does a tool rise above all others in its field but, as a fan of quality craft and design, I appreciate this object. Its build, versatility, and functionality are all exceptional. Yes, it's expensive, but if you grind a lot of pepper, and expect to do the same in the future, you'll appreciate the investment.

Note: In barbecue, black pepper interacts beautifully with fat, sinking in and almost merging to form the bark. However, on briskets, I don't use *freshly* ground pepper. I instead prefer a pre-ground pepper that has aged and mellowed a bit (see page 113).

RAGS AND TOWELS As with tongs and beer, so with rags and towels: you can never have too many. Wait, what? A piece of foldable cloth is a magical implement, good for everything from cleaning up spills to grabbing heavy slabs of meat to picking up hot irons or wiping off a knife. Just buy a pack of twenty-five. You can launder and reuse them until they fall apart, and if one gets soiled beyond repair, it's not a big deal to toss it.

SHEET PANS AND SIZZLE PLATTERS I keep stacks of full-, half-, and quarter-size sheet pans around to serve many functions: as a plate for drying out a steak in the fridge, to transport items between the kitchen and the outdoors, as a baffle in a smoker, and to receive freshly cooked items and their drippings. They are as tough as nails, both freezer- and oven-friendly, and very easy to clean.

The same can be said for sizzle platters, which are little steel or aluminum dishes that you may have seen in restaurant kitchens. These can be purchased inexpensively at a restaurant-supply store and serve much the same function as sheet pans. They're smaller but just as tough and will happily sit under a broiler. I've even been to sophisticated restaurants that serve food on them!

SPRAY BOTTLE This is not intended to cool you off on a hot day, but that could be pleasant unless it's filled with apple cider vinegar, as mine often is. I usually have a couple of spray bottles, one containing vinegar and the other water, within reach. Spraying your ingredient at the end of a smoke, before it's taken out or wrapped, moistens the exterior, extending the time the food can smoke and helping it cook to just the right moment without drying out.

THERMOMETER I'm an instant-read-thermometer junkie, especially the model called Thermapen, which I heartily endorse. It's the most expensive thermometer out there, but also the quickest, most accurate, best designed, and easiest to use. I always have at least two, if not three, on hand.

A good digital meat thermometer won't really help you determine when brisket or ribs are perfectly done, because doneness on those cuts is somewhat independent of temperature. But knowing internal temperatures provides useful information along the way. A thermometer is also invaluable for checking doneness on such shorter-cooking items as prime rib, tomahawks, pork steaks, poultry, and fish. The speed of the instant-read function is crucial because you only want to have the smoker door open for a very short time while cooking.

There are also ingenious options for checking temperature (connected via Wi-Fi to your phone or an external unit) where you never even have to open the smoker lid. For instance, we tried the popular MEATER device and liked how one end of the thermometer goes into the meat and the other end senses the ambient temperature around the meat. It also tracks the temperature readings and charts over time for a quick record of your cook. Although the MEATER is very clever and useful, I am usually staring at fire, so pulling out my phone to open the app every time I need to check a temperature is highly inconvenient. And anyway, I think I'm set in my ways, enjoying the simplicity of an old-school (digital!) thermometer.

TONGS In an interview with *Bon Appétit* magazine, Marie Kondo, author of *The Life-Changing Magic of Tidying Up*, answered a query about keeping one's kitchen neat by saying, "Most people have too many tongs!" My response is "Can you ever have *enough* tongs?" (Stacy's response: "Do you really need all these tongs?")

But seriously, I use tongs constantly when I'm cooking outside. I have different sizes, from small ones for precision jobs to extra-long, heavy-duty ones. I use them to turn food but also to reach into a fire and grab a burning log. Indeed, on every cook, I have one pair for handling things inside the smoker or on the grill and another pair for going right into the firebox to arrange and rearrange the architecture of coals and logs.

I've found that the extra-long, heavy-duty tongs from a restaurant-supply store are pretty good. But, gee, wouldn't it be cool if someone made some great ones to their own specs? *(Hmmm. . . . . . .)*

107

WORKTABLE When you're plotting out your outdoor kitchen, be it a bougie patio affair or a makeshift setup in the dirt around a campsite, do yourself a favor and plan for a table or other elevated, flat working area. Just as counter space always seems to be in short supply in a home kitchen, it's in even higher demand outdoors where ingredients are going on and off grills and tools, sauces, mops, sprays, seasonings, towels, drinks, kids' toys—you name it—are looking for a spot to rest. When I go camping, the first thing out of the truck is a folding table. I recommend you do the same and set up either a temporary or permanent work area at your house.

BUILDING FLAVOR

On weeknights, or even weekends, when you've been out all day and need to get dinner ready in a hurry, having a well-stocked cupboard of rubs, condiments, and sauces speeds the delivery of tasty, umami-rich meals. You can buy this stuff or you can make your own, customizing flavors and spice levels to your taste. The great thing is that they last a good long time, so a little effort up front can mean big time savings later on, not to mention the delicious satisfaction of having done it yourself.

Rubs

Fresh seasonings can be great, but it's super-handy to have spice rubs in the pantry, whether you're prepping for a long smoke or just want to add some hassle-free flavor to something you're about to grill. For this reason, Franklin now manufactures a few basic rubs. Our BBQ Spice Rub is our own (somewhat) less salty take on the iconic Lawry's Seasoned Salt. Our Steak Spice Rub is an umami bomb with universal applications that just bumps up the flavor of everything. And our Brisket Spice Rub, which is a mix of the classic salt and pepper I've always advocated, also makes a good foundation for your own additions.

When I'm first learning how to cook something or developing a new technique, I start with kosher salt as my sole seasoning. Then once I know that my process is solid, I build flavor from there. I truly believe that by the end of an hours-long smoke, what you ultimately want to taste is meat, smoke, salt, and pepper. But that doesn't mean I won't keep messing around with different spice blends for the rubs or new flavors for our slathers (like French's yellow mustard or hot sauce) with the hope that a little extra complexity might make our customers happier.

The fifty-fifty combination of salt and pepper that we use is still unequivocally the best and most reliable seasoning for brisket, ribs, or whatever you want to smoke. It's our foundation. So if you're just starting your brisket game, begin with a basic salt-and-pepper rub and then, if you want to mess around with additional flavors, add a layer of something else, like all-purpose BBQ Spice Rub. (But take it easy on the sugar, as it burns at higher temperatures.)

On the following pages are my guidelines for assembling your own basic seasonings. I'm not exactly offering the recipes for the Franklin rubs, but I am giving you the general framework. Creating rubs at home gives you control of the ingredients, saves you a few bucks, and allows you to find the formulas that suit your own palate.

BBQ SPICE RUB

Lawry's Seasoned Salt is an American classic, and I've always appreciated it as such. In fact, when I was growing up, my dad put Lawry's on almost every steak he ever grilled, so it also has a taste of nostalgia for me. As you know, I'm a tinkerer, and I like to custom make things when possible, so following is a list of the most prominent ingredients (in order of volume) that go into our all-purpose BBQ Spice Rub. This is an homage to Lawry's—with a little less salt.

Use with: Practically everything, but notably on chicken, steaks, and chops, or mixed with salt and pepper for brisket, beef ribs, and baby back ribs. But you can really use it on anything you like, as it's that versatile.

—

Makes as much as you want

- Fine sea salt
- Garlic powder
- Onion powder
- Paprika
- Mustard powder
- Mushroom powder
- Celery powder
- Lemon powder
- Granulated sugar

Rubs such as this should be made to satisfy your own taste, which is why I don't offer volumes for each ingredient. You could make this à la minute to sprinkle on some chicken breasts you're about to cook up, or you could make a larger volume to last for a while. The base of most rubs is salt, garlic powder, and onion powder. I recommend starting with equal parts of those and adding in amounts of the other, more specialty flavors, like mushroom or mustard powders, in smaller quantities and to taste. Ultimately, combine all of the ingredients to taste and mix well. Store in an airtight container in the pantry for up to 3 months.

Variations: Other possible additions include vinegar powder, tomato powder (be careful, as it can burn), and Worcestershire powder.

STEAK SPICE RUB

We created this rub to be an umami booster for almost anything you put it on—similar to old-style BBQ seasonings but without any MSG.

Use with: I sprinkle this rub on everything from steaks to pasta sauces; it delivers just that extra bump of deliciousness. For steaks, use this on larger cuts that cook at lower temperatures (like prime rib), as it can scorch at high temperatures.
—
Makes as much as you want

- Sea salt
- Garlic powder
- Onion powder
- Mushroom powder
- Tomato powder
- Mustard powder
- White pepper
- Granulated beef stock
- Worcestershire powder
- Mustard powder
- Celery powder

Again, start with the base of equal parts salt, garlic powder, and onion powder. Then add the other ingredients in smaller amounts to taste. In a bowl, combine all of the ingredients and mix well. Store in an airtight container in the pantry for up to 3 months.

Variations: Other possible additions include brewer's yeast, dehydrated parsley powder, and apple cider vinegar powder.

BRISKET SPICE RUB

A one-to-one ratio (by volume, not weight) of coarse salt and 16-mesh ground black pepper makes up our foundational brisket seasoning, but you can also use this mixture to start building any kind of rub you want.

Fermentations and Pickles

The only flavor as compelling as acidity in any dish is umami. Fermentation and pickling are two excellent ways to obtain both of these elements at the same time. If you don't already practice these simple ways of building flavor by making delicious condiments, you should definitely consider starting. These recipes require minimal labor and very little active prep. Time itself does most of the work, along with our little friends, the microbes.

SAUERKRAUT, TWO WAYS

I always have a jar or two of sauerkraut on hand. There's something about its tart flavor, prickly acidity, and fermented funkiness that takes the heaviness out of a rich smoked piece of meat. Best of all, it's very easy to make at home, which—without fail—yields a more complex, delicious, and healthful version than what comes in a can. (Canned sauerkraut undergoes pasteurization, which kills all the beneficial probiotics obtained during fermentation.)

Use with: Kraut is always good on a hot dog, of course, but it's wonderful served alongside Firepit Pork Shoulder "Steaks" (page 133) or Baby Back Ribs (page 199). Indeed, it's even good with Smoked Duck (page 207). Serve it chilled, or warm it up gently with some of the meat juices from the cutting board to give it a little extra heft.

—

Makes 1 quart

Equipment
- Kitchen scale
- Bowl
- Muddler (or some sort of implement such as a pestle or wooden spoon for pressing down hard)
- One 1-quart or two 1-pint widemouthed mason jars
- Rounded glass weights
- Fermentation lids (depending on number of jars)

Fermentation lids can be purchased online, where you'll find a number of brands, all of which work well. These are not required for making sauerkraut or any other fermented foods, but they do keep your ferment nice and neat. They are a type of air lock, allowing carbon dioxide to escape without letting oxygen in. This makes it harder for mold or other bacteria to grow on top of the kraut. Although almost anything that might grow there is harmless, it is neither appealing to look at nor to think about, so I discourage such growth by using the lids.

The glass weight—a thick, glass disc—can be placed on top of the cabbage at the end to keep it submerged in the brine.

SOPRANO SAUERKRAUT

You can make wonderful sauerkraut with nothing more than cabbage and salt, but I like to bump up the complexity and the high notes by adding a bit of garlic and ginger. You can really add any sort of additional seasoning you like. Caraway seeds are classic, but spicy chiles or dill would also be nice.

- 1 head green cabbage
- Kosher salt
- 2g piece fresh ginger, finely minced or grated on a Microplane
- 1 large garlic clove, finely minced or grated on a Microplane
- Distilled or spring water for topping if needed

Using a large chef's knife, halve and core the cabbage, then slice the halves into a thin julienne. A fine shred improves the fermentation dynamics.

Tare a bowl on the kitchen scale and then weigh the cabbage. Determine what 2.5 percent of the weight of the cabbage is and add that amount of salt. For instance, if you have 800g of cabbage, you'll add 20g of salt. (If you want a saltier kraut, feel free to up the percentage of salt. Keep in mind that anything more than 5 percent can be painfully salty, and the fermentation process may not work as well.)

Add the ginger and garlic to the bowl and, using your hands, thoroughly mix everything together. Pound the cabbage a bit with a muddler to speed the process of drawing out its liquid. Let the mixture sit for 30 minutes at moderate room temperature to allow the salt to draw moisture out of the cabbage. While the cabbage sits, sterilize the jar(s) by boiling them in a pot of water for 10 minutes, then (carefully) transfer them to a clean kitchen towel.

After 30 minutes, begin to fill the prepared jar(s) with the damp cabbage. After each addition, use the muddler to press on the cabbage, compacting it against the bottom of the jar. As you work your way up, you want the cabbage to be tightly and densely packed. Stop when the cabbage reaches 1 to 1½ inches from the rim of the jar. Pour in any liquid remaining in the bowl. As you pressed down on the cabbage, enough salt water should have naturally released from it to cover the contents of the jar. If you don't have quite enough, add a splash of distilled or spring water to submerge the cabbage completely.

Press the contents down with the glass weights and seal with the easy-fermenter lid(s). Set the jar(s) in an open container, such as a Tupperware bowl, to catch any liquid that overflows due to expansion during fermentation. Place your jar(s) and container in a dry, dark, room temperature spot.

Within a day or two, you should see tiny bubbles rising to the top when you tap the side of the jar(s). That means the fermentation has started. After 7 to 10 days, feel free to open the lid and taste. You should have a mild-flavored sauerkraut. For more intense earthy and funky flavors, let the sauerkraut go for more time, up to 3 weeks. When the kraut has achieved a flavor you like, suspend the fermentation by putting the whole jar in the refrigerator. The sauerkraut will keep in the fridge for up to 1 month.

FENNEL AND RADICCHIO KRAUT

This version of sauerkraut combines the refreshing bitterness of radicchio with the anise-flavored lift and added crunch of fennel. The purple cabbage and radicchio combine to turn the mixture a stunning deep purple.

- ½ head radicchio
- ½ head purple cabbage
- 1 fennel bulb
- ½ teaspoon fennel seeds
- Kosher salt
- Distilled or spring water for topping if needed

Using a large chef's knife, halve and core the radicchio and cabbage. Slice the halves into a thin julienne. With the knife, remove the stalks from the fennel bulb, then cut the bulb in half lengthwise and gently remove the core. Now slice it crosswise, matching the size and texture of the purple ingredients. Slice off several of the fennel fronds and peel off the tiny leaves. Mince the tiny leaves finely and reserve about ¼ cup.

Tare a large bowl on the kitchen scale, combine the vegetables in the bowl, add the fennel seeds, and then weigh the vegetables. Determine what 2.5 percent of the weight of the vegetables is and add that amount of salt. For instance, if you have 950g of vegetables, you'll add 24g of salt. (If you want a saltier kraut, feel free to up the percentage of salt. Keep in mind that anything more than 5 percent can be painfully salty, and the fermentation process may not work as well.)

Using your hands, thoroughly mix everything together. Pound the vegetables a bit with a muddler to speed the process of drawing out their liquid. Let the mixture sit for 30 minutes at moderate room temperature, continuing to allow the salt to draw moisture out of the vegetables. While the vegetables sit, sterilize the jar(s) by boiling them in a pot of water for 10 minutes, then (carefully) transfer them to a clean kitchen towel.

After 30 minutes, begin to fill the prepared jar(s) with the damp vegetables. After each addition, use the muddler to press on the vegetables, compacting them against the bottom of the jar. As you work your way up, you want the vegetables to be tightly and densely packed. Stop when the vegetables reach 1 to 1½ inches from the rim of the jar. Pour in any liquid remaining in the bowl. As you pressed down on the vegetables, enough salt water should have naturally released from it to cover the contents of the jar. If you don't have quite enough, add a splash of distilled or spring water to submerge the vegetables completely.

Press the contents down with the glass weights and seal with the easy-fermenter lid(s). Set the jar(s) in an open container, such as a Tupperware bowl, to catch any liquid that overflows due to expansion during fermentation. Place your jar(s) and container in a dry, dark, room temperature spot.

Within a day or two, you should see tiny bubbles rising to the top when you tap the side of the jar(s). That means the fermentation has started. After 7 to 10 days, feel free to open the lid and taste. You should have a mild-flavored sauerkraut. For more intense earthy and funky flavors, let the sauerkraut go for more time, up to 3 weeks. When the kraut has achieved a flavor you like, suspend the fermentation by putting the whole jar in the refrigerator. The sauerkraut will keep in the fridge for up to 1 month.

FERMENTED HOT SAUCE

Homemade hot sauce is a truly satisfying project that's also really tasty. Yes, there are tons of great hot sauces available on store shelves—more than ever before, it seems—but when hot chiles are in season in the summer, I like to buy them by the bushel and make sauce from my own combinations.

You can make a tasty hot sauce just by stewing chiles in vinegar and spices, then pureeing and straining the result into bottles. But fermenting the chiles first brings a complexity and umami that I find irresistible.

This recipe is for a basic chile hot sauce, but you can add other flavors and ingredients to your heart's content. Ferment your chiles with garlic or other vegetables, for instance. Or add fresh garlic post-fermentation before you puree. Put your chiles on the smoker or grill to add some of the flavor of the fire. Herbs and spices always have a place too. Fruits, like mangoes, pineapples, and berries, can also play a role. Add vinegar or mezcal to the puree for even more complexity. Getting creative with your sauces is half the fun.

Use with: All savory foods!

—

Makes 1 quart

Equipment

- 1-quart widemouthed mason jar
- Kitchen scale
- Rounded glass weight
- Fermentation lid
- Fine-mesh strainer
- Funnel (optional)
- Sauce bottles (optional)

If you already own the quart jar and lid described for fermenting sauerkraut (see page 115), you have all you need to ferment chiles for hot sauce. (Be sure to sterilize the jar before filling it, as you did for the kraut.) The strategy is slightly different, though, as you'll start with a brine. You'll also need a strainer and, if you want to be able to dash out the sauce onto your food, recycled sauce bottles.

BASIC PEPPER SAUCE

Use any kind of chiles you like or a mix of varieties. The fresher they are, the better. If you want a milder sauce, remove the seeds. The colors that your sauces achieve can be electric. Combine yellow, red, and orange varieties for brilliant shades, or stick with green chiles, like jalapeños and serranos, for an alluring green sauce. A standard brine for successful fermentation ranges from a 2 to 5 percent salt solution. I like mine on the less salty side, between 2 and 2.5 percent. (Salt can always be added later.) That's about 6g of salt for every 240g (1 cup) of water. Use your scale to make the calculations.

- Water, as needed
- 1 to 2 pounds organic chiles, stemmed
- Fine sea salt
- 2 garlic cloves
- White wine vinegar for pureeing (optional)

Estimate how much water you'll need to submerge the chiles once they are packed into the 1-quart jar. Tare a bowl on the kitchen scale, then weigh the water. Multiply the water weight by 0.02 for a 2 percent salt solution (or whatever percentage you wish) and add that amount of salt. Stir to dissolve.

Pack your stemmed chiles into the sterilized jar. You can cut them in half, but don't bother chopping as they'll be pureed anyway. Crush the garlic cloves and add to the mix.

Pour the salt brine into the jar, covering the chiles completely and leaving about 1 inch of headspace in the jar. Press the contents down with the glass weights so the chiles are completely submerged and give the jar a gentle shake or stir to work out any air bubbles. Seal the jar with the fermentation lid.

Store the jar in a dry, dark spot at moderate room temperature (anywhere from 65° to 80°F will ferment the chiles very evenly and thoroughly).

Within a day or two, you should see tiny bubbles rising to the top when you tap the side of the jar. That means fermentation has started.

After a week or two, feel free to open the jar and take a whiff. The fermentation funk will get stronger the longer you leave the chiles, so if you like just a light earthiness, consider taking them out now.

Once you've deemed your chiles ready, drain the contents of the jar through a fine-mesh strainer, capturing the brine in a bowl. Puree the contents in a blender or food processor with a little bit of the brine or any other liquid to taste. If you use water, it will dilute the flavor a little. Vinegar will give it that classic sharpness and also significantly slow down the ongoing fermentation process. A lot of vinegar will mostly kill the fermentation. If you want a completely shelf-stable sauce, boil it on the stovetop for about 10 minutes to kill the active bacteria. This process also changes the flavor a bit, making it a bit less intense and aromatic.

Strain the puree through the fine-mesh strainer into a bowl, reserving the solids. Now you can adjust the consistency to your liking. If your sauce is a little too thin, stir in some of the solid matter from the strainer. If it's too thick, strain it again to remove more of the solids. Your sauce should be thick enough to remain a mixed solution without separating too much but thin enough to dribble through the top of your sauce bottle. Simply store the sauce in the mason jar or use a funnel to fill your sauce bottles.

The sauce will keep in the fridge for up to 3 months.

PICKLED VEGGIES

Good ol' dill pickle slices are a classic condiment for Central Texas barbecue (as are raw onions), and you can guess why. The intense and unctuous flavor of long-smoked meats desperately needs something to cut it, and pickles have the piercing acidity and sharp flavor that both moderate the richness of the meat and refresh your palate for the next bite, just like a sip of wine or beer might do.

I find that pickles go with everything, and that's how we use them at the restaurant. They dress up a meal and can serve as either condiment or side dish. It's pretty much a core principle of Franklin Barbecue to have pickles at the ready, as we do at home with fermented hot sauces, sauerkrauts, and kimchi.

You can make fermented pickles by following the brine instructions given with the Basic Pepper Sauce (page 119). Those vegetables will indeed get very funky. But for everyday pickles, I preserve vegetables in a seasoned vinegar solution for a day or two—sometimes even a few hours is enough—to get the effect I want.

You will need a 1-quart mason jar with a lid and a rounded glass fermentation weight (or some other form of weight) to keep the pickles submerged. All sorts of vegetables can be pickled. I tend to favor carrots, fennel, onions, radishes, green beans, shallots, and cucumbers. As with hot sauces, you can create a multitude of flavors by adding spices, herbs, and garlic and by using flavored vinegars.

Here's my basic process, using fennel as the main ingredient. (By the way, pickled fennel made it onto the cover of *Franklin Steak*, but we forgot to include the recipe there. People email about this more often than you'd think. So here it is!)

Use with: Smoky, rich meats and rich, fatty fish.
—
Makes a scant 1 quart

- 1 cup / 230g rice vinegar
- ¼ cup / 200g granulated sugar
- 1 teaspoon / 4g kosher salt
- 1 large fennel bulb
- 10 black peppercorns

In a small saucepan over medium-high heat, combine the vinegar, sugar, and salt and warm through, stirring to dissolve the sugar. Do not allow the mixture to boil, as you don't want the liquid to reduce. Remove from the heat.

While the vinegar mixture is heating, prep the fennel by trimming off the stems and fronds from the bulb, then halving it lengthwise, removing the core and then thinly slicing crosswise on a mandoline or with a knife.

Put the peppercorns into a 1-quart jar and then pack the fennel on top. Pour the hot brine over the fennel and place a glass weight on top to keep it submerged. Leave the jar on the countertop with the lid set loosely on top until the brine cools to room temperature. Tighten the lid and refrigerate the fennel for at least 3 hours or up to 1 day before serving.

The veggies will keep in the fridge for up to 1 month.

Sauces

I'm a traditionalist at heart and truly revere the original folks who cooked barbecue and ran the small-town restaurants where it came into its own. Thus, I've always respected the fact that, traditionally, Central Texas barbecue has never employed sauces. Not only is this practice in tune with the sort of bare-bones, hardscrabble style of the people who settled this area and cooked their own version of barbecue, but it is truly the best way to show respect for the art of slow-smoking meat. Woodsmoke, itself, is a complex ingredient and a wonder to experience, with a little salt and pepper, as it interacts with the flavor of the meat.

That said, people love sauces. And by your third or fourth unadorned bite, a little bit of tang or acid, sweetness and spice definitely enlivens the palate. I like to serve my sauces on the side so people can indulge as much or as little as they like.

Over the years, I've come up with a number of sauces that I love. Most of these can be mixed and matched with any type of protein, so don't think that because I paired one sauce with a certain dish here it doesn't go just as well with something else. (And if you're looking for the recipes for our barbecue, espresso, and vinegar sauces, check out the *Franklin Barbecue* book.)

RYE BBQ SAUCE

I do like rye whiskey, I must admit. Hence, it has made it into various sauces I've thrown together over the years for dinners and events and all kinds of cooks. The basic idea is that rye and cherries go together really well (hey, Manhattan cocktail) and are even better when combined with black pepper and fatty meats. This recipe is a distillation of all those ideas. Pick your favorite not-very-sweet rye whiskey for this; I often use High West Double Rye. This is a pretty sweet sauce, so if it tastes too sweet to you, back off on the jam a bit.

Use with: BBQ chicken, pork ribs, and pork steaks.
—
Makes about 4 cups

- 1 cup / 320g cherry preserves
- 1 cup / 275g ketchup
- ½ cup / 115g apple cider vinegar
- 3 tablespoons / 20g freshly ground black pepper
- 2 tablespoons / 12g garlic powder
- 2 tablespoons / 12g onion powder
- ½ cup / 100g Worcestershire sauce
- 4 tablespoons / 65g tomato paste
- 2 tablespoons / 30g Dijon mustard
- 1 cup / 200g dry rye whiskey

In a medium saucepan over medium heat, combine the preserves, ketchup, and vinegar and warm through. Pour the hot liquid into a blender and puree until silky smooth. Pour the mixture into a 1-quart jar.

Add the pepper, garlic powder, onion powder, Worcestershire, tomato paste, and mustard to the jar and whisk until smooth. Let the sauce cool to room temperature, then add the whiskey and stir to combine. Taste and adjust any flavors as you like, then cap and refrigerate.

The sauce will keep in the fridge for up to 6 weeks, serve as soon as you can.

SPICY BBQ SAUCE

Most barbecue sauces are laden with spices but are rarely actually spicy. This one is—or at least it can be as spicy as you want it. The sweetness is balanced in the background, so you don't really notice it. The secret to a good spicy sauce is the spicy part, not the base, which makes preparing a sauce like this super-easy.

As a base, I simply use Franklin's standard barbecue sauce, or one that I think would take well to some spicing up, and augment from there. I like a Tex-Mex kind of sauce where the heat comes from Mexican chiles, but you could also mix up a version with Thai bird chiles, sriracha, or whatever you like. Because chiles vary in heat, flavor intensity, and water weight, this is a preparation that needs to be done by taste and to taste.

Use with: I love a tangy, sharp, spicy sauce with brisket, pork ribs, and, especially, chicken.

—

Makes as much as you want

- 1 cup / 100g jalapeño, serrano, habanero, and ancho chiles or a mix of your favorite hot chiles
- 2 cups / 450g your favorite barbecue sauce

In a blender or food processor, puree the chiles, adding a splash of water or vinegar if it needs extra liquid to form a puree. In a medium bowl, add the barbecue sauce and slowly add 1 to 2 tablespoons of the chile puree to start, stirring well to combine. Taste it right away, but also let it sit for about 15 minutes and then come back to retaste, as it can take a little while for the heat and flavors to integrate. For more chile pepper impact, add more puree incrementally until it gets to the right balance. If it was too much pepper to start, add a little more sauce to mellow it out.

I like sauces and condiments for their versatility.
After all, who wants to spend all of their time

Use with: Al ...

but it's espe ...
Half Shell (page 147).

Makes 1 cup

- ½ cup / 115g grapeseed oil
- 1 tablespoon / 7g Hungarian sweet paprika
- 1 tablespoon / 9g Aleppo pepper flakes
- 1 teaspoon / 2.5g ground guajillo chile
- 6 garlic cloves, finely chopped
- 1 bunch flat-leaf parsley, leaves plucked and finely chopped
- 3 tablespoons / 20g finely chopped shallot
- ½ cup / 115g olive oil
- 4 tablespoons / 45g sherry vinegar
- Finely grated zest of 1 lemon
- 1 teaspoon / 4g kosher salt

In a small saucepan over low heat, combine the grapeseed oil, paprika, Aleppo pepper, and ground guajillo chile, stir to combine, and let infuse for about 30 minutes. Stir in the garlic and let it warm for 3 minutes. Remove the pan from the heat and allow the mixture to cool slightly.

In a medium bowl, combine the parsley, shallot, olive oil, vinegar, and lemon zest. Pour in the warm peppery oil and stir with a spoon. Adjust the salt, as needed, to taste.

Pour the chimichurri into a jar, let cool, cover, and refrigerate for 1 to 2 days to allow the flavors to develop before using.

The sauce will keep in the fridge for up to 2 weeks.

6

—

OPEN FIRES

Home Cooking on the Firepit and the Grill

There's almost nothing I like better than camping with my family. While we don't necessarily rough it, we love to get out of the city and into the hills and forests far from the noise of traffic, leaf blowers, and the surprisingly loud chatter of the spandex-clad cycling groups that pedal constantly past our Austin home.

Stacy likes to note that our camping meals aren't what you might expect on a typical camping trip. "It's not like we just open a can of biscuits or throw hot dogs on the grill," she says. However, cooking and eating a good meal in nature is one of the finest pleasures in life, so we eat well whether we're camping in a mountain forest or grilling on the firepit in our backyard.

This chapter is devoted to re-creating the often-primitive style of camping-trip cooking at home. The recipes require neither bells and whistles nor advanced techniques, but I do have some ideas that will enrich your meals, improve flavors, and take your campfire cooking to a satisfying place.

This is a good time to make use of the whole fire. After all, if you were fully out in nature, the fire is the only heat source you would have, so it makes sense to capitalize on every aspect of it. And while I love to coax all the energy, flavor, and nuance out of a fire, I don't always want to have the aggressive flavors of smoke or ash in every bite. Hence, some of the flavors I'm going for in this chapter are subtly smoky and some are not smoky at all. Good flavor and texture begin with prep, which is why many of these recipes include salting (dry brining) and drying out for a day or more before cooking.

I use different aspects of the fire to cook vegetables. You can char any tough green vegetables such as broccoli, brussels sprouts, or green beans over the hot flame of a chimney or in a roaring fire. I tend to like my vegetables rather undercooked, meaning I don't mind if they have a bit of crunch. Cooking larger vegetables directly in the coals is a surprisingly wonderful and low-effort way to fill the table.

As for proteins, there are a few things that I like to cook over direct and indirect heat on a firepit (pork steaks and côte de boeuf), as well as some hybrid smoking-grilling dishes on the PK grill (chicken and fish), which offers the best of both worlds. Finally, see the recipe for Jordan's Perfect Green Salad (page 169) for a simple and delicious accompaniment to every meal.

FIREPIT COOKING

The elements of firepit cooking are primitive: wood, flames, grill. The unbridled nature of fire often leads to extremes. If you are timid about cooking over open fire, you won't maximize the opportunities it presents. Don't content yourself with only hot dogs and s'mores or go all in when the flames are at their peak and either under-cook or burn your food—or do both at the same time.

Firepit cooking rewards patience and nuance. Once you learn these skills, you can cook just about anything well. For that reason, I love to cook larger cuts of meat on the firepit. They can take a while—up to a few hours of careful tending—but when done well, they give you the best of cooking over hot coals: grill action and a bit of smoke at the same time.

Getting Started

First, have plenty of wood on hand that is sized to fit your firepit. If you've got a big, open area, full-size fire logs work fine. But if it's a smaller space, you'll want to split those logs and maybe cut them shorter so you can feed the fire without making it stumble. As with all of the cooking in this book, avoid softwoods, like pine and cedar, just as you would in your smoker. Oak, fruit and nut woods, and hickory are all excellent. For more on selecting wood, see chapter 3.

Obviously, don't build a fire—whether it's in your backyard or in a park somewhere—when it's dangerously hot, dry, or windy. Even in perfect weather, it's wise to have water at the ready from a live hose with a spray nozzle or a couple of full buckets in case the fire starts to get away from you. I also keep fire blankets on hand—one in the camper and a small one in my cooking kit.

The best firepit cooking is anchored by a strong coal bed, so when you finally start cooking, the fire is on its second or third round of logs (the initial logs having burned down to establish that bed).

If you have charcoal and a chimney, it's perfectly fine to start the fire that way, as the two generate quick and durable heat. I often place my prepped chimney in the center of the firepit and surround it with two or three stacked logs on three sides. I then light it and, after about twenty minutes, the heat and flame generated by the smoldering charcoal begin to escape the chimney and ignite the logs. This way, you get a jump on burning the wood while the charcoal provides an instant mini–coal bed to get you started.

After your first logs are going, dump and remove the chimney (place it somewhere safe) and use a long set of tongs to rearrange the logs in a log-cabin formation (see page 83) to encourage airflow and combustion. As those first logs start giving up some hot coals, add another log or two and wait. When those burn down, you should have an ample coal bed for cooking. After this, maintain the firepit so it has one or two burning logs and a good coal bed. This is how you always want your firepit set up for cooking.

The trick to cooking over a firepit is tending and managing the fire along with whatever you're cooking. It's a little more difficult to control a fire versus adjusting the flame of your gas stove's burner, but the general principle is the same. Only in this case, you adjust the logs and coals to produce the optimal heat and smoke you want.

To have precise control, use a pair of extra-long tongs to constantly move logs around and rustle up the coals. You can prepare a nice, flame-free coal bed to cook over while maintaining your gently burning logs on the side.

Prepping the Grate

For the recipes that follow, you need a good-size grate to cover the firepit. In the best of all worlds, it shouldn't cover the entire surface of the firepit (mine covers half) because you need to have access to the logs and coals. Make sure your grill is clean and give it a quick wipe with grapeseed oil before putting food on it.

Be sure to have a comfortable distance between the grate and the coals. You want it close enough to get plenty of heat but not so close that you can't escape the heat. It should also be high enough so the fat can drip down without creating flare-ups. A grate that is sixteen to eighteen inches above the coals should do the trick.

One of the beauties of firepit cooking is that you can achieve a hybrid of grilling and smoking. The fact that you're cooking over a ton of wood coals is significant—they provide the delicious smoke that you can't get from charcoal. But because the "smoke chamber" is simply the wide-open sky, foods can cook for a long time without taking on too much smoke.

In this chapter are a few things—both meat and vegetables—I love to cook on the grate and in the coals of the firepit. These are terrific ways to take full advantage of the whole fire.

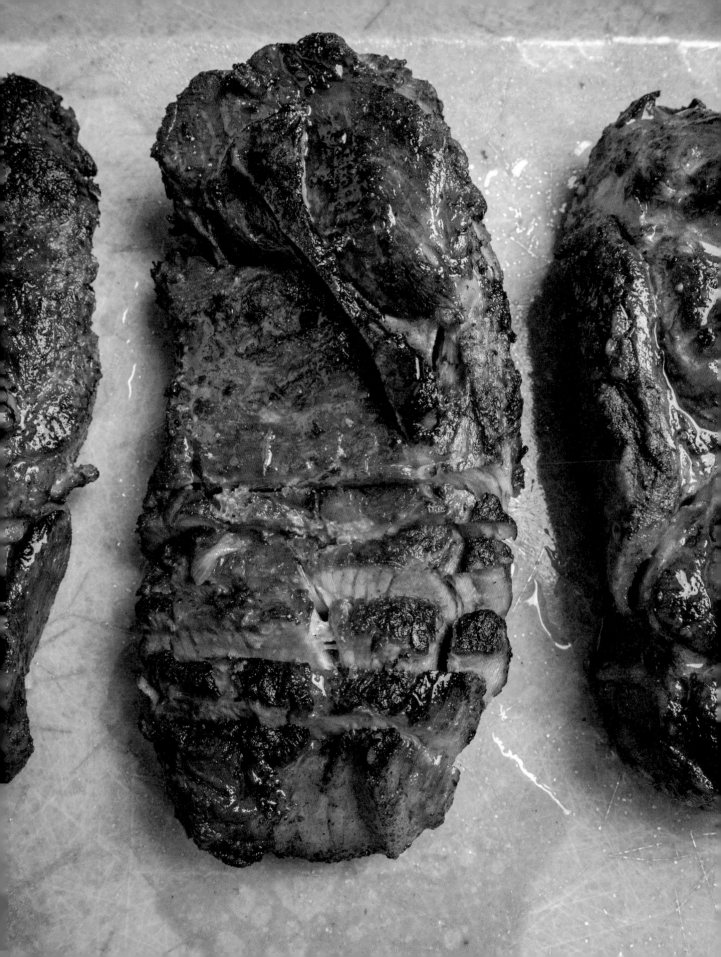

FIREPIT PORK SHOULDER "STEAKS"

This preparation of pork combines the dynamics of a slow cook with the fast grill, producing a flavor that hearkens to both. Pork steaks absorb the delicious effect of the grill as their drippings vaporize on the hot coals and subsequently rise up to perfume the meat. Yet they also pick up gentle smoke from the coals and burning wood.

While this pork is cooked like a steak or a chop, it is actually cut from the shoulder, aka the pork butt. As you know, the meat from the shoulder is much tougher than meat from the loin, where the chops are. Consequently, pork shoulder is usually cooked long and slow to break down the collagen and make the meat pull-apart tender. The goal for this approach to shoulder steaks is to cook them over direct heat, like a pork chop, but slowly and deliberately so they soften a bit over time. You're not looking for exceedingly tender, pulled-pork consistency here. But you're also going to cook well past medium-rare as you might do for a chop. The length of the cook allows the meat to pick up precious flavor from the fire.

Speaking of pork chops, they would be equally delicious cooked over the firepit and basted with the mop recipe listed here, but they are an entirely different muscle—from the loin, not the shoulder—which cooks quite fast, should be served at a lower internal temperature, and doesn't need all that time to break down tough muscle fiber. Cook thick-cut pork chops as you would a steak (though not as rare), but feel free to baste them with this mop for added flavor.

THE MEAT

I recommend using rich, well-marbled pork, as the fat content helps the meat hold up over a long cook. Definitely try to avoid modern, conventional pork, which has been purposely bred to be lean. I look for heritage breeds such as Berkshire or Red Wattle. There's even a ranch raising Ibérico pigs in Texas, the same breed that produces the world's greatest jamón in Spain.

Use a bone-in pork butt and ask your butcher to cut it into steaks two to three inches thick. You could also buy a whole shoulder (more affordable but also more work) and then break out the old bone saw, which I sometimes do much to Stacy's chagrin (not her favorite thing to find lying around the kitchen), and cut through the bone yourself. Most of the steaks from a pork butt will have a sliver of the blade bone in them. This is what you want. Boneless butts have to be butterflied to get the bone out and then are tied up in a round. This is fine for roasting a whole piece, but the steaks need to retain their structural integrity and thus must retain the bone.

THE MOP

A mop is necessary here to add pork-friendly flavors and to keep the meat moistened so it doesn't burn while it cooks for a good long while over the coals. The mop also provides additional fat that your pork might not have (even a well marbled heritage breed), augmenting the supply of vaporized juices as it drips onto the coals.

You can prepare the mop on the stovetop in advance and then warm it over the fire when it's time to use. Doing this advance prep makes it easy to cook these steaks at home or at a campsite.

Cook time: 3 to 4 hours
—
Makes 4 to 6 servings

- Kosher salt
- One 6- to 8-pound / 2700 to 3600g bone-in pork shoulder butt, cut into 2- to 3-inch-thick steaks

The Mop
- 1½ pounds / 350g unsalted butter
- ⅓ pound / 150g thick-cut bacon, in one piece, cut into chunks
- 3 cups / 690g apple cider vinegar
- Peel of 1 orange
- Peel and juice of 1 lemon
- 15 to 20 garlic cloves, smashed (use the larger amount if you favor garlic)
- ½ yellow onion, coarsely chopped
- Grapeseed oil for the grate

Liberally salt the steaks on both sides and set them on a baking sheet. Let the steaks air-dry, uncovered, in the refrigerator for at least 1 day or up to 2 days.

To make the mop: In a medium saucepan over low heat, combine the butter, bacon, vinegar, orange peel, lemon peel, lemon juice, garlic, and onion and

warm until the butter melts, stirring occasionally. Keep the mop warm on the grate.

Build a firepit fire, burning down six to eight logs to create a nice coal bed, then maintain another couple of logs burning on the side to supply coals. When it's time to start cooking, clear the burning logs off the coal bed so you have just coals to cook over. The logs can continue to burn on the side. Because of the length of time that these steaks cook, they are best done over a medium- to low-heat coal bed with the grate set eighteen to twenty-four inches above the coals. Oil the grate.

Remove the steaks from the fridge and lay them on the grate. Don't temper the steaks, just put them on cold, as the first couple of hours are really about developing the exterior of the meat.

Since the steaks are going to cook in the open air for the next 1½ hours or so, set the fire to mellow and let 'em rip. Stand by with tongs and flip the steaks every now and then to develop a nice, rich crust. As the fire progresses, bring in fresh coals from the burning logs on the side and keep the meat moving so it never flames up. You want these steaks to be kissed by heat and the clouds of their own evaporations, not by flames.

After the first couple of flips, starting 15 to 20 minutes in or when you see the surface of the steaks beginning to dry out, start to mop to keep the surface moist. Gently drizzle the mop over the tops of the steaks. It will drip down and hiss in the coals, which is a good thing! Turn the steaks and mop the other side. Repeat this every 10 minutes or so as needed to keep the surface moist. Also, be careful with your mop—you need it to last the whole cook and then have some to put in the wrap, so go easy.

Now you're about 2 hours in. Much as with brisket, you need your crust to get a little crustier than you ultimately want it because it will be softened after you wrap. When you've built a great crust, it's time to wrap the steaks in aluminum foil. Have a foil sheet ready for each steak. Remove the steaks, place each one on a foil sheet, and pour a little bit of the mop over the top. Wrap each steak tightly in the foil and return the steaks to the fire for about 1 hour more.

Using a digital thermometer, test for doneness; the steaks are ready to remove from the heat when the thermometer inserted into the side of each at the middle reads about or just above 200°F. Allow the steaks to rest while you add

some wood to replenish the coal bed. This could take 40 minutes to 1 hour.

Once your coals are back up and hot—or you're simply ready to eat—unwrap the steaks and put them back on the grate to sizzle up the surface and regain your crust. Save the juices retained in the foil to pour over the sliced meat.

Remove the steaks from the fire and, when cool enough to hold, it's time to slice and serve.

FIREPIT CÔTE DE BOEUF

A staple of French cookery, côte de boeuf is immensely versatile. The term basically refers to a bone-in rib-eye steak, as we call it here in the US when it's just one bone. It's typically cut thick in France and meant to feed two people. It could also be known as a (very short) standing rib roast. But rib roasts are usually cooked in the oven, and here I use a two-bone rib steak to create a sort of hybrid steak–prime rib dish. You could also use a thick-cut, single bone rib eye, but it would cook faster. The pleasures of prime rib roast and grilled steak converge in one piece of meat: plenty of tender interior meat is matched with a thick, crunchy crust that supplies the ideal contrast of smoke, salt, and caramelization. Plus, one big rib steak is plenty to feed two to four people, making for a lovely presentation that can be shared family-style.

Cook time: 2 to 3 hours
—
Serves 4 to 8

THE MEAT

Any good butcher can prepare a two-bone rib steak for you, though it's wise to order it a day or two in advance to make sure he or she can cut it to your preference. If the steak has an especially thick outer layer of fat, ask the butcher to trim some off to avoid flare-ups. You may also want to ask that the steak be tied with butcher's twine so it maintains its form during a fairly lengthy cook, though I usually skip this step. Prep involves little more than dry brining with salt.

Côte de boeuf is a natural for the firepit, which allows you to cook directly, indirectly, and with a bit of smoke—all from fresh wood coals. The thickness of the cut demands a relatively long cook and gives you lots of flavor from the fire. This is basically a low-pressure two- to three-hour cook—the kind of thing you do while waiting for friends on a Saturday afternoon. Ideally, cook it slowly to get even cooking throughout. But because it is steak, you can also cook over higher heat if you need to speed things up.

- Kosher salt
- 2 two-bone rib steaks, trimmed and tied
- Water, beef stock, or vinegar for spritzing
- Melted tallow or grapeseed oil for coating
- Horseradish Cream Sauce (recipe follows) for serving
- Grapeseed oil for the grate

Liberally salt the exterior of the steaks and set them on a baking sheet. Let the steaks air-dry, uncovered, in the refrigerator for 24 to 36 hours.

Build a firepit fire, burning down six to eight logs to create a nice coal bed, then maintain another couple of logs burning on the side to supply coals. When it's time to start cooking, clear the burning logs off the coal bed so you have just coals to cook over. The logs can continue to burn on the side. Because of the length of time that these steaks cook, they are best done over a medium- to low-heat coal bed with the grate set eighteen to twenty-four inches above the coals. Oil the grate.

While the first logs are cooking down, remove the meat from the fridge to temper it a bit before putting it on the fire.

Stand the steaks vertically on the bone on the grate. This heats up the bone and begins the process of slowly cooking the adjacent meat. After the bone is browned, turn the steaks onto a side and let them go from there. Don't turn the spinalis side (the rib-eye cap or muscle that runs along the outside of the steak, opposite the bone) to face the flames from the burning logs. The spinalis is the most tender and flavorful part of the rib eye. It will always cook past rare, but it's good to protect it from too much heat so it retains its moisture.

Keep the steaks over low to medium heat on the cooler areas of the grate. Move them around fairly frequently, flipping them at the same time. While you're flipping, also keep a spray bottle full of water handy to spritz the steaks, cool the sides, keep the crust from drying out too much, and prolong the cook. Slowly build a crust on the side facing the heat and then flip the steaks to let that side cool while the other side cooks. Do this repeatedly until a digital thermometer inserted into the side of each steak at the middle reads 110° to 112°F. At that moment, pull the steaks off the grate.

Allow the steaks to rest while you add some wood to replenish the coal bed until it is raging hot. After the steaks have rested no less than 30 minutes and for up to 1 hour—however long it takes to get the fire really hot again—gently coat the steaks in the tallow and throw them back on the grate for a couple of minutes on each side, until the crust gets nice and sizzling again. Remove the steaks from the heat.

When the steaks are cool enough to hold, it's time to slice and serve. Slice between the bones so you have two rib-eye steaks. Slice the meat off the bone, leaving the bone in place, thus retaining the shape of the original steak. Then cut across the steaks, fanning from the bone to obtain nice long strips. Arrange the slices on a platter and include the bones. Serve horseradish sauce alongside.

HORSERADISH CREAM SAUCE

Makes 1½ cups

- 1 cup / 240g sour cream
- ⅔ cup / 140g prepared horseradish
- 2 tablespoons / 28g champagne vinegar
- Grated zest of 1 lemon
- Fine sea salt

In a medium bowl, combine the sour cream, horseradish, vinegar, and lemon zest and mix well. Season with salt. Cover and chill for at least 1 hour before serving. The sauce will keep in the fridge for up to 2 weeks.

ADDING A HINT OF SMOKE

To get a whiff of smoke flavor when grilling with charcoal, add a little wood to the mix to combine the radiative heat of coals with the gentle complexity of woodsmoke.

In my second book, *Franklin Steak,* a framework was described in which a whole log is inserted lengthwise into the back half of a grill, dividing the grill into two zones. Named the Franklin Formation by Jordan, the half over the log is a cool zone, while the front half, containing lit charcoal, is a hot zone. The front edge of the log catches fire, creating some smoke and flames. This produces a sort of hybrid grilling and smoking situation.

In the interim, I have made some improvements to the original framework (although, honestly, it still works well). By putting the log in the back of the grill, you had to reach over hot coals any time you wanted to put anything on the cool zone. Lately, I've been playing around with wood lengths and placements and tried putting the log in different orientations (which Jordan jokingly named the "Franklin Reformation" and the "Franklin Reformation Variation Orientation"). Terminology aside, the following ideas are just different configurations of a good technique.

First, you want to cut the log to ten inches or so, which gives you much more flexibility. You can then insert the wood perpendicularly into the grill relative to the grill's length, set it at an angle, or position it parallel to the length in the middle, allowing hot coals to smolder it on two sides and creating a cooler zone in the center. Using a smaller log offers quite a bit more adaptability than the original formation—and provides the same benefits.

When choosing logs, I look for ones that are particularly dense and squarish in shape with no bark. I like these blocky logs because those with a wedge or a tip will catch fire on that end and burn too rapidly.

Whereas the cool zone of the original formation was rather long and narrow without much room to avoid the flaming edge of the log, this new version is both more comfortable and more adjustable. Like a slider on a mixing board, you can move the log in tighter to create a concentrated coal bed and large cool zone, or you can move it away from the charcoal to give the coal bed a wider birth, diminishing the intensity of its heat while maintaining a bit of smoke and a good-size cool zone. All in all, this is a much smarter configuration, and all that's required to add a hint of smoke is sawing down your firewood to the right size for your grill.

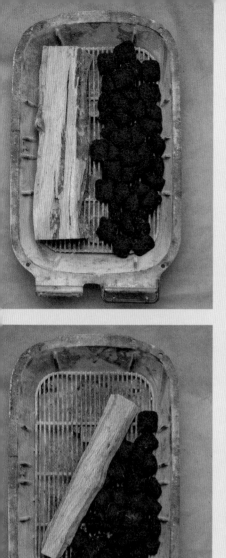

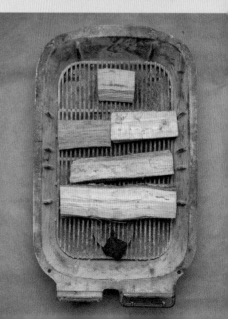

OUR FISHY FRIENDS

I'm not very good at cooking fish on the grill, which may be the reason I don't do it nearly as much as I could. Like everyone, I worry about all kinds of details particular to our fishy friends: the tiny bones that you have to remove from the raw fish, the cooked fish before you eat it, or your mouth after you've taken a bite; the scales that can slice and dice your fingers; and the skin that, no matter how hard you try, always seems to stick to the pan or the grill, mangling your fillet.

All that said, one thing is undeniable: fire-cooked fish done well is simply delicious. And certain fish love the kiss of the coals. Their flavors work almost as well as beef with a smooch of smoke. So, in recent times, I've set about to cooking fish and other sea delicacies on the grill, trying to replicate and even improve on the bites that I've had in the past.

REDFISH ON THE HALF SHELL

I've been trying to master the technique of cooking fish "on the half shell" since having redfish served this way at an event a few years ago. In coastal Texas and eastward through Louisiana and the Carolinas, half-shell cooking—leaving the fish scales on—is famously practiced on redfish, also known as red drum. Redfish is popular among sport fishers for being a very wily prey; it doesn't stop fighting even once it's been brought to shore and subdued. Also, its scales are famously sharp and numerous, making it a dangerous thing to handle.

The idea behind half-shell cooking is so full of common sense that it's easy to underrate. When we buy fish at a store, the scales have almost always been already removed because they are difficult and messy to deal with at home. But scales also make the fish skin inedible. Of course, with this method, you can't eat the skin (and for those of us who love Japanese delicacies such as crispy salmon skin, this is a loss), but the hard barrier formed by the scales accomplishes three things: (1) it prevents the skin from sticking when it's cooked directly on a hot surface like a grill; (2) it prevents moisture loss to the base of the fillet, leaving a tender, flaky version of fish at its best; and (3) it prevents too much smoke from invading.

You can cook nearly any fish—cod, haddock, trout, salmon—this way with excellent results. In fact, I don't see myself messing around with skin in the future and will instead ask my fishmonger to leave the scales intact.

This is a perfect grill for the family or small gatherings.

I've worked with the technique some and have a method for doing it. It involves covering the fillets with a large, preheated cast-iron pan so the top of the fish cooks in tandem with the underside. This method would work just as well on a firepit.

Cook time: 12 to 15 minutes
—
Serves 4 to 6

- 2-pound redfish fillet, with skin and scales intact
- Grapeseed oil for rubbing
- Kosher salt and freshly ground black pepper
- Red Chimichurri (page 125) for serving

Set the fish on a baking sheet and let air-dry, uncovered, in the refrigerator for 1 to 2 hours. This helps the top to brown during cooking.

In the meantime, get your charcoal chimney going to create a medium-hot coal bed in your grill—not blistering but also not about to die. If you like, add a log using the perpendicular Franklin Formation (see page 142) to generate a bit of smoke and subtly flavor the fish. (If you're using a PK grill, make sure the hinged side of the grate is over the coals, as you'll need to access them later.) You can also just use charcoal. Place a very large cast-iron skillet on the grate directly over the coal bed to preheat.

When your grill is ready, remove the fish from the fridge and rub the flesh side of the fillet with grapeseed oil, salt, and pepper. (Even though the scale side doesn't necessarily need it, I rub oil and salt on this side, too, to make doubly sure the skin doesn't stick to the grate.)

Oil the grate and lay your fillet, scale-side down, over the cool zone (not directly over the coals) so the thick end of the fillet lines up with the coal-facing side of the log.

Place the heated skillet over the fillet, making sure that one edge of the skillet also sits above some live coals. The idea is to funnel some of the heat and smoke from the coals and the log over the top of the fish. There's enough heat coming from below to cook the underside of the fish. Using tongs, grab about ten lumps of hot charcoal and place them on top of the skillet.

After about 10 minutes, carefully peek under the skillet to see how the fish is progressing. Using a fish spatula, pull the fish off the grill when a digital thermometer inserted into the thickest part of the fillet reads 135° to 140°F. When you pick up the skillet, drop the coals back into the grill.

Transfer the fillet to a platter, top with the chimi-churri, and serve immediately.

GRILLED, SMOKED WHOLE BRANZINO

Most good fishmongers have a nice supply of whole fish, but few people seem keen to buy and cook them. I was one of those people—until now.

There are great reasons to buy a whole, cleaned fish: you can see quite clearly that its integrity is intact; you get to enjoy all of its meat, from the cheeks to the belly; you don't have to remove the bones; it's very easy to cook; and it makes a nice shareable dinner for multiple people (depending on the size of the fish).

Leaving a fish intact helps it cook slowly and evenly on the grill. Of all the whole fish that I've grilled, I have consistently found that the well-known branzino, which is native to Mediterranean waters, is wonderful flavored with smoke from wood coals. You could also use trout, grouper, sea bream, or bass, but the buttery flavor of branzino combines deliciously with the sweet edge of the smoke.

When you purchase the fish, ask the fishmonger to leave the scales intact. Scaled fish tends to stick, even to the aluminum foil that I use for this method. The goal here is to get tender flesh, not crispy skin.

I love the classic preparation of fish stuffed with lemon slices, fennel, and parsley. While it may seem as though you need a special occasion to warrant cooking a whole fish, this is a no-fuss preparation that can be done quickly, inexpensively, and effortlessly on a summer weeknight. Deploying a piece of wood in the Franklin Formation (see page 142) provides just a kiss of smoke.

Cook time: 13 to 20 minutes

—

Serves 4

- 2 whole branzinos (about 12 ounces / 350g each), cleaned, with scales intact
- Grapeseed oil for rubbing
- Kosher salt
- Fronds from 1 fennel bulb (use the bulb to make pickled fennel)
- 1 lemon, thinly sliced, plus lemon wedges for serving
- 1 bunch flat-leaf parsley
- Pickled fennel (see page 120) for serving

In a large bowl, combine water and ice cubes to prepare an ice bath. Rinse the fish under cold running water (work carefully to avoid cutting yourself on the scales), then place it in the ice bath until you're ready to grill.

Ready a chimney half to three-fourths full of charcoal, then dump the charcoal into the grill bed. Using tongs, arrange a Franklin Formation with the log parallel to the length of the grill and in the middle so you can surround it on three sides with coals. You don't want the grill to be roaring hot, so use just a few pieces of charcoal on each side.

Remove the fish from the ice bath and carefully dry each one with a clean kitchen towel. Rub the fish all over with the grapeseed oil and very gently salt the flesh. Dividing them evenly, stuff the fennel fronds, lemon slices, and parsley inside the fish cavities.

Cut two squares of aluminum foil; you will lay each fish in a foil boat, so be sure the squares are big enough to accommodate the size of your fish. Fold each foil square in half. Using a sharp spike or the tip of a knife, poke six small holes in the center of the foil—the area that will be the boat's bottom.

Place a fish in the middle of the foil, spine near the holes, and fold the sides of the foil up into a little open-topped boat shape, pinching the ends together to form the bow and stern. (Technically, you could do this without foil, but the foil makes the fish easier to handle.)

Lay the foil boats on the grate directly over the log (the cool zone), with the fish spines facing in toward each other. Cook until the meat starts to firm up to the touch a little, 8 to 10 minutes. Flip each fish within its boat and cook for 5 to 10 minutes more. The length of time depends on how hot your grill is and the size of the fish. Remove the fish from the grill when the flesh appears flaky but still moist when tested with the tip of a knife or prong.

Transfer the fish to a large platter and serve with lemon wedges and pickled fennel.

DEVISING AN OYSTER GRILL GRATE

When I couldn't find a grate specifically built for grilling oysters, I decided to fashion one myself! The idea was to make medium-size gaps in a grill grate so the "cup" of an oyster would fit snugly and not tip over and spill its juice while I'm gently cooking the oyster over hot coals. In this case, I modified a PK grate using bolt cutters and pliers. I made only seven slots, because by the time the oysters have cooked and then cooled enough to handle, they should be sloshed down and you should be getting a fresh round started.

OYSTERS WITH SHALLOT-CHIVE BUTTER

The act of buying and shucking oysters may seem like something that only happens at restaurants, but it turns out that shucking an oyster is only a minor challenge and becomes even less so the more often you do it. (I wouldn't want to do hundreds a night, but a dozen at home is no problem.) On top of that, oysters are an incredibly wholesome, hearty, and nutritious food that travels well. Delicious when served with wine, beer, and cocktails, oysters are a good change up if your home dining habits need some fresh ideas.

While I love the clean, crisp bite and salty rush of raw oysters, grilling them with a compound butter is revelatory. A little pat of butter placed on an oyster on the half shell quickly melts into the brine as the oyster gently cooks to tender perfection. The magic is in that mixture of butter and brine, which, in the confines of the shell, creates a tiny bit of buttery oyster bisque. Nothing could be simpler and more appealing.

The only challenge is to shuck the oysters and get them on the grill without spilling too much of their liquor. I do recommend shucking them first. Some people let the fire open the oysters for them—putting an unshucked oyster over the coals will eventually boil the oyster and release the adductor muscle that holds the shell closed. But, often as not, the brine boils and blasts the shell open, shattering some of the calcium and spilling the brine. You want a clean shuck and a gentle cook. Don't worry if you spill a little of the liquor when placing the oysters on the grill. As long as its shell is pretty

level, the oyster will release more briny liquor as it cooks, providing plenty of liquid in the shell to mix with the butter.

Although you won't go through a whole stick of butter with only a dozen oysters, it's easier to make the compound butter in quantity, and it keeps well in the refrigerator for later use. Incidentally, feel free to riff on the compound butter mixture, as almost any herb or spice works. Even plain butter is delicious. Just be sure it's unsalted butter because the oyster brine itself contains plenty of sea salt. A splash of hot sauce is a wonderful way to finish off each oyster.

Cook time: 20 minutes (including making the compound butter)

Serves 2 to 6 depending on number of oysters

- ½ cup / 110g unsalted butter, at room temperature
- 2½ tablespoons / 8g finely minced fresh chives
- 1 tablespoon / 10g finely minced shallot
- 12 to 36 raw oysters in their shells
- Hot sauce (see page 97) for serving

In a small bowl, combine the butter, chives, and shallot and mix well. Spoon the butter in a uniform line down the center of a sheet of plastic wrap or aluminum foil. Fold one long side of the sheet over the butter and, using a straightedge (such as a ruler), press against the butter while pulling on the lower part of the sheet to force the butter into a uniform log about 1 inch in diameter. Wrap the butter in the plastic wrap or foil, twist the ends closed, and refrigerate to firm up. Leftover compound butter will keep in the fridge for up to 2 weeks.

Ready a chimney full of charcoal, then dump the charcoal into the grill bed and spread out the coals.

Shuck twelve of the oysters and gently set them on a platter. Remove the butter from the refrigerator and unwrap. Using a knife, cut off small slices of butter and place one atop each shucked oyster.

Gently place the oysters on the grate directly over hot coals. The liquor will start to simmer and melt the butter. When the butter has completely dissolved into the liquor, after 1 to 2 minutes, depending on the heat of your fire, use tongs or kitchen tweezers to remove the oysters from the heat and place them on a platter.

Allow the shells to cool enough to handle, then eat the oysters while still warm, topping each with a dash of hot sauce. Once you've slurped down a few, get started shucking the next dozen oysters for round two.

SMOKED CHICKEN

While working on this book, I discovered that Aaron never cooks with the lid of his PK grill closed, which I do all the time. Practically, this means that Aaron doesn't smoke foods on the PK, and I do. (All the other recipes for the grill in this chapter should be cooked without the lid.) This is probably because Aaron co-owns a restaurant that has a number of smokers and has at least one at home, while for the longest time I did not. And because of his preference for the perfect smoke that a fully burning fire creates, he's never even thought of smoking anything on the PK, which offers a more rustic, less efficient smoking environment but still works quite well for smaller items such as this chicken.

Every time that I serve a smoked chicken to guests, they all say, "Wow, I never thought of smoking chicken." Nothing seems more obvious to me, and, in fact, I can think of almost no more delicious way of cooking chicken. Smoking delivers not only beautiful golden brown skin with a ton of flavor but also incredibly tender, juicy meat. And the method could not be simpler. By the way, this method works equally well for quail, guinea fowl, Cornish game hens, or any other small- to medium-size bird with light-textured meat. It also produces wonderful boneless leg of lamb, pork roasts, and any other medium-size cut that will fit on the grill with the lid closed.

While you can easily do a whole intact chicken this way, I recommend spatchcocking (aka butterflying) it so it cooks more evenly

and faster and thus doesn't take on too much smoke. Basting it with a vinegary mustard solution adds zest and character.

Basic spatchcocking is quite easy. You can make it more complicated if you decide to remove the wishbone and ribs, which requires a smidge of deft knifework. But I like to leave the ribs on to protect the breasts during cooking. Plus, they're much easier to remove when the bird is cooked. The wishbone is a little tricky to extract, so I usually just cut it out after the bird comes off the grill. As always, the chicken tastes and cooks better if it has been pre-salted and air-dried in the fridge for at least a day. —Jordan

Cook time: 50 to 80 minutes

Serves 4 to 6

- Kosher salt
- 1 whole chicken, 3 to 5 pounds, spatchcocked

The Mop
- ½ cup / 120g sherry vinegar
- ¼ cup / 55g unsalted butter
- 2 tablespoons / 30g Dijon mustard
- 1 tablespoon / 20g honey
- 1 tablespoon / 9g freshly ground black pepper
- ½ teaspoon / 3.5g kosher salt

Liberally salt the chicken all over and set it on a baking sheet. Let the chicken air-dry, uncovered, in the refrigerator for at least 24 hours or up to 72.

To make the mop: At some point before cooking the chicken (this can be done a day ahead of time, then refrigerated and reheated), in a small saucepan over low heat, combine the vinegar, butter, mustard,

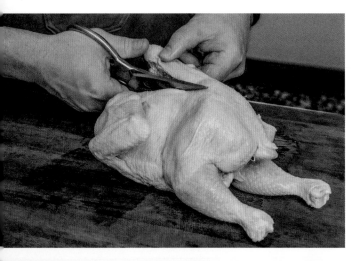

honey, pepper, and salt and warm through, stirring occasionally, until the butter melts and the mixture has formed a sauce.

Remove the chicken from the fridge and allow it to temper on the counter.

Ready a chimney full of charcoal, then dump the chimney into one end of the grill bed. Using the Franklin Formation (see page 142), lay a log next to the coals to form the boundary of a two-zone setup, or alternatively, place a good-size wood chunk on the coals. Close the lid and allow the wood to start smoking. The temperature should be hot—somewhere between 400° and 450°F.

Lay the chicken, breast-side up, on the grate as far as possible from the heat, with the legs nearest to the heat. Close the lid and cook for 25 minutes.

Open the lid, lift the chicken (using tongs or pick it up with a kitchen towel in your hands), and place a quarter sheet pan under the chicken. The pan will capture your mop and let it combine with the chicken juices, evaporating them and steaming the underside of the bird. This is a good time for the first drizzle with the mop. Drizzle with the mop again after 15 minutes and a third time after another 15 minutes.

Now's a good time to gauge the temperature. Insert a digital thermometer into the center of the breast (you're looking for about 150°F) and then in the thickest part of the thigh, but not touching the bone (you want 175° to 180°F). It will probably require more cooking, so continue to baste every 10 to 15 minutes until it's done.

When the chicken is done, transfer it to a platter and let rest until cool enough to carve and serve.

VEGGIE SIDES AND MAINS

Vegetables are wonderful beings, and I love them a lot. As much as my career has been defined by the cooking of meat, my own eating life has always included a ton of veggies. And when I'm cooking out, it's often handy to cook my vegetables over the fire.

Firepit cooking allows you to cook several ways at the same time. While your pork or beef steaks are slowly cooking on the grate above the fire, you can pull aside some coals or burning logs to quickly prepare some appetizers or side dishes. Or you can cook sturdy vegetables right down in the coals.

These same simple techniques can easily be adapted for use in a charcoal grill too. Although the firepit conveys the added benefit of real woodsmoke, I don't want the vegetables to take on too much smoke, and most of the time they don't. A hint of smoke is nice on your vegetable accompaniment, but if you've already got smoky meats, too much might be overkill. Also, I'm not at all against cooking up these vegetables in the fire and making a giant spread for a meal unto itself!

GRILLED MUSHROOMS

Mushrooms are some of the easiest and most natural vegetables to cook on the fire, and they add an earthy, complex flavor to meals as a side dish, as a garnish to meat, or as a delicious meat substitute if you're feeding vegetarians. While they are light and seemingly flimsy, mushrooms are actually quite resistant to high heat and fire, giving them the ability to take on gentle grill or smoke notes.

Cultivated mushrooms available in bulk at good grocery stores tend to be fairly well cleaned and manicured. If you detect any soil or leftover matter from their growing medium, simply wipe it off with a damp towel and trim off the bottom of the stems. Never wash mushrooms under water, as their spongelike bodies will soak up the moisture and become damp and slimy.

The ideal mushrooms to grill are whole portobellos, large trumpet mushrooms, and, especially, clumps of maitake mushrooms, also known as hen of the woods. In nature, maitakes grow at the base of trees and reach sizes up to twenty pounds. But they're also easily cultivated, which is what you normally find at grocery stores. They grow in soft, feathery clumps that are more robust than they seem. You can pull apart the clusters into smaller bite-size strands or leave them attached in big clumps, as I do when roasting them over coals.

Cook time: 20 minutes
—
Serves 2 to 4

- 1 pound / 450g maitake, portobello, or trumpet mushrooms, wiped clean and trimmed as needed
- Grapeseed oil for brushing

Using fresh, hot wood coals in a firepit or glowing-red charcoal in a grill bed, spread out the coals so you have a wide area for grilling. You want fairly high heat, as mushrooms can take a lot as they cook down. Also, they absorb a lot of smoke flavor—almost too much at times—so fast cooking helps them not take on too much.

Put the mushrooms on a baking sheet and gently brush them with grapeseed oil.

Place the mushrooms directly on the grate over high heat and grill until tender, 10 to 15 minutes, depending on the heat of your fire. Maitakes take a bit longer; you want the edges to get a little crisp and begin to dry out. You'll be impressed with how much heat mushrooms can take.

Remove the mushrooms from the heat and serve immediately.

FIRE-KISSED BRUSSELS SPROUTS

I could eat brussels sprouts just about every day of the week, and I love doing them on the fire. The intense heat from the flames and coals tempers the bitterness of the sprouts while adding a layer of charry complexity. To finish, I toss in something a little sweet, like thinly sliced apples, pomegranate seeds, or halved grapes.

Brussels sprouts are convenient to cook on a fire that you already have going for a larger protein, and they roast equally well over the wood coals of an open firepit or the glowing charcoal in a grill. You want the brussels sprouts as cold as possible before putting them on the fire, so keep them in the refrigerator or on ice until just before cooking.

To cook down sprouts in the fire, you can use a perforated grill pan or even a cast-iron skillet, but I have had the best luck using an inexpensive metal fry basket purchased from a restaurant-supply store. The metal on these baskets tends to be heavy-duty, so they can take the intense heat and wear and tear.

You can use this method in a firepit over wood coals or over charcoal in a standard grill or even quickly over a charcoal chimney. And it works well for green beans, parcooked fingerling potatoes, cauliflower, broccoli, and any other sturdy, fibrous vegetable you might want to try. Their water content and fibrous character allow them to resist the heat of the fire long enough to pick up just enough charry taste to be delicious.

Cook time: 10 to 15 minutes

Serves 2 to 4 as a side dish

- 1 pound / 450g brussels sprouts, trimmed, halved, and well chilled
- Grapeseed oil for coating
- Kosher salt
- Juice and grated zest of 1 lemon
- 1 cup / 140g pomegranate seeds
- Apple cider vinegar for drizzling

Create an open bed of exposed coals. Then take two fresh logs and place them on the coals as a stand for the fry basket. Push the logs together tight enough to compact the charcoal so there are no major air gaps that could generate flames.

In a medium bowl, toss the brussels sprouts with just enough grapeseed oil to coat evenly and lightly and then season with salt.

Dump the brussels sprouts into a fry basket and reserve the bowl. Place the basket directly on the coals. Grasp the handle of the basket almost immediately and begin flicking your wrist to toss the sprouts gently so they don't become too charred. Continue tossing as the sprouts develop a lightly charred exterior. You want to prolong the cook as much as possible until it seems the sprouts are going to burn without ever getting to that point. You are cooking the exterior while keeping the interior crisp.

When the sprouts are ready, remove the basket from the fire and return the sprouts to the bowl. Add the lemon juice and mix well. Add the pomegranate seeds, lemon zest, and a drizzle of vinegar and mix.

Serve the sprouts immediately, as they get soggy quickly.

COAL-ROASTED VEGGIES

As long as you use the appropriate vegetables and take them off the fire at the right time, there's no easier way to cook vegetables than to put them directly on the coals. Instead of steaming them in a pot, they cook in their own juices, which concentrates their flavors.

Thin-skinned vegetables, like eggplants, definitely pick up some smoke, so be prepared for smoky baba ghanoush (the way it was meant to be). But thick-skinned vegetables, like gourds and squash, can take a lot of heat and will cook beautifully without getting particularly smoky. Onions and cabbages can be cooked without wrapping them in aluminum foil, and although their exterior will obviously blacken, you'll find a beautifully cooked interior when you remove the charred outer skin or leaves. They can also easily be wrapped in foil and steamed with full protection from the flames.

However you do it, the ability to cook vegetables on a fire that you've already got going to cook a major protein not only is poetic but also saves time, heat, labor, and steps (our kitchen is a fair distance from the backyard firepit, so roasting veggies in the oven while cooking outside requires a lot of schlepping and diverts attention). If you have a wood fireplace, and it's a cold winter night, you could even use that. You can also successfully cook eggplants on charcoal in a grill, but they'll lack the sweet flavor of woodsmoke. Whichever method you choose, you want hot, active coals.

SMOKY EGGPLANT BABA GHANOUSH

Cook time: 20 minutes
—
Serves 4 as an appetizer or side dish

- 2 medium globe eggplants
- 1 small garlic clove, finely chopped
- Extra-virgin olive oil for serving
- 1 lemon, halved
- Kosher salt
- Toasted bread slices or crackers for serving

Tuck the eggplants into the sides of the firepit, around the smoking coals. You can brush some coals on top of the eggplants too. Within 5 to 10 minutes, the eggplants will begin to shrivel and the skin will become crunchy. If you haven't covered them with coals, use tongs to turn the eggplants so the upward facing side goes into the coals. Try not to manipulate the eggplants too much, as you don't want to break the skin and release all the juice.

After about 20 minutes, the eggplants' skins should be shriveling and crisped. They should have cracked a little and will be lightly leaking juices into the coal. Using tongs, gently transfer them from the fire to a big bowl or platter and let them cool. They'll release a lot of liquid as they sit.

When they eggplants are cool enough to handle, cut them in half with a knife and use a spoon to scoop out all the flesh into a medium bowl. Remove any pieces of burned skin, as it will deliver an acrid taste. While the flesh is still warm, add the garlic. Then pour in a little olive oil, squeeze in the juice from a lemon half, season with salt, and mix until well combined. Taste and adjust with more olive oil, lemon juice, and salt as needed. Let sit for 5 to 10 minutes to allow the flavor of the garlic to mellow in the heat.

Serve the baba ghanoush warm, with toasted bread.

COAL-FIRED SQUASHES AND ONIONS

Cook time: 30 to 40 minutes

—

Makes as much as you want

- White, yellow, or red onions
- Acorn, butternut, or other winter squashes
- Extra-virgin olive oil for serving
- Unsalted butter for serving
- Flaky salt
- Fresh lemon juice for serving

Literally the easiest dish in the world to make, this involves nestling whole onions and squashes into the edge of the fire among the coals, then leaving them for 30 to 40 minutes. The onions will blacken and tenderize, which is how you know when to pull them out. The squashes will also carbonize on the outside, but a few pokes to gauge tenderness will tell you when they're done.

Let the onions cool on the outside before peeling. Serve as you wish. For instance, they're delicious as a side when cut in half and topped with a little butter and flaky salt. Likewise, allow the squash to cool enough to handle, then cut in half and scoop out and discard the seeds.

Serve the squash with topped with a little olive oil, butter, salt, and lemon juice.

FIRE-STEAMED CABBAGE

Cook time: About 30 minutes

—

Serves 4 to 6 as a side dish

- 1 head red or purple cabbage
- Unsalted butter for topping
- Kosher salt and freshly ground black pepper
- 2 or 3 slices bacon (optional)

Cut the cabbage in half but don't core it. Lay the halves, flat-side down, on a cutting board and mold a piece of aluminum foil tightly around each piece, leaving a little extra foil for a lip (which makes for easy handling). Flip the halves so they are cut-side up. Top each half with a pat of butter and season with salt and pepper. Place the cabbage halves, foil-side down, in the hot, active coals.

If you have a grate that sits over the coals, roll the bacon slices, if using, together into a coil and place it on the grate directly over the cabbage so the delicious pork fat will drip down onto the slowly cooking cabbage.

The cabbage is ready when it appears soft and moist. This should take about 30 minutes, depending on the heat of your coals. Transfer the cabbage to a platter and serve immediately.

JORDAN'S PERFECT GREEN SALAD

One thing that I have in common with all of the Franklins (Aaron, Stacy, and their daughter, Vivian) is that hardly a day goes by that I don't eat a salad. Salads are everything that barbecue is not: fresh, raw, green, crunchy, acidic, and not too filling. When we're test cooking, I am often tasked with making a simple green salad for dinner because we need something wholesome and satisfying—even though the dressing is just oil and vinegar and salt.

There's not exactly a trick to my method, just a few things that I do always seem to provoke compliments. Here's my basic theory of salad, along with a couple of variations that use what you might have on hand or be inclined to eat on any given day.

THE KEYS TO A PERFECT GREEN SALAD
- **A mix of fresh, tender lettuces, washed and fully dried**
- **Very good extra-virgin olive oil**
- **Vinegars and citrus**
- **Salt and pepper**
- **Restraint**

Lettuces

I like to make a blend of two or more different varieties of lettuces, choosing from such types as butter lettuce, romaine, arugula, dandelion, and endive. Mostly, I love a little crunch. If you are starting with uncleaned lettuce, always wash and dry it fully using a salad spinner (something every kitchen should have). Wash and spin dry the leaves about 20 minutes ahead of dinner and let them chill in the fridge for the perfect condition. The leaves must be free of any dampness or the dressing will not adhere.

Very Good Extra-Virgin Olive Oil

Top-quality extra-virgin olive oil cannot be beat. It has a richness and complexity that you won't get from any other type of oil. I recommend that you splurge on a bottle from Italy that might set you back thirty dollars or more. It will last a long time if you use it sparingly. I use mine pretty much exclusively to finish proteins and for salad dressing.

Vinegars and Citrus

I use all kinds of vinegars, but my standard is the trio of red wine, white wine, and sherry vinegars, which I use interchangeably, depending on my mood. Occasionally I use balsamic vinegar, but it's somewhat sweet. You can also use fresh citrus juice in addition to or instead of vinegar. Sometimes I split this component of a dressing between the citric acid of a lemon and the acetic acid of vinegar, as each kind of acid imparts a slightly different tang, adding another dimension.

Salt and Pepper

It's easiest to add salt by the pinch. Be careful not to use too much, as you can always add more. Just a little bit brings out the flavors of the greens, oil, and vinegar. Too much obscures them. A couple quick twists of the pepper grinder should be sufficient. As with salt, you don't want too much.

Restraint

Even slightly overdressing it can make a salad vaguely off-putting. Too much vinegar and the acidity is too cutting. Too much oil and the salad is greasy. Too much dressing in general and the lettuces get soggy. Go as light as possible at the beginning and add a touch more dressing only if needed.

TECHNIQUE

When you have great lettuces, just a little oil and vinegar applied directly to the leaves can be enough. Most vinaigrettes call for oil and vinegar in a three-to-one ratio, but I find that less vinegar is preferable when you're using a great olive oil. I mix them together by feel, but you might start by trying a four-to-one or even five-to-one ratio.

Right before I serve the salad, I pour some olive oil on the lettuces. Use less than you think you need, then add just a light drizzle of vinegar and a pinch each of salt and pepper and gently toss together with freshly washed hands. Make sure every leaf gets coated with oil. If some didn't, add more oil. Taste a leaf and let your palate decide if the dressing is just right or if you need a few drops more of either oil or vinegar.

Variations

Premade vinaigrette: To make a vinaigrette ahead of time, follow the preceding principles, but combine the ingredients in a small bowl or jar with a healthy dollop of Dijon mustard (more than you think you might want), which allows the dressing to emulsify. Add a pinch of salt, an even smaller pinch of sugar, and a few twists from a pepper grinder, then whisk everything until the mixture has a nice, thick texture that will coat the leaves. Some of my other favorite additions include finely minced garlic, minced shallot, and fresh dill or tarragon, finely chopped.

Salad additions: Add whole leaves of fresh flat-leaf parsley, mint, or basil to your lettuce mix. They always lift a salad. Also, very fine slivers of onion contribute a nice little background jolt. If you're serving the salad in a wooden bowl, rub a clove of garlic onto the wood before adding the lettuces to give the perfect garlicky accent. A bit of crunch can also be nice: chopped radish, sliced cucumber, or chopped celery. Don't add more than one or two of these additional ingredients to a salad. A green salad should be almost invisible compared to the rest of the food—that is, until everyone remarks on how perfectly it is dressed.

HERBY BUTTERMILK POTATO SALAD

I've been making this rich, creamy potato salad for years, as it goes great with just about anything, especially intensely grilled meats such as the Firepit Côte de Boeuf (page 139). The cool, slightly sour heaviness of the buttermilk and sour cream provide a soothing contrast to the smoky, crusty surface, and the herbs add some lift and zing. Best of all, it's really easy to make and to customize to your own taste. This is a large portion, but the leftovers keep well in the fridge for a few days, during which it will almost certainly get eaten.

Makes 3 to 4 quarts

- 6 pounds Yukon gold potatoes, diced into ½-inch cubes
- ¼ cup / 12g fresh dill, finely chopped
- ¼ cup / 12g fresh chives, finely sliced
- ½ cup / 30g fresh parsley, finely chopped
- 2 cups / 400g mayonnaise
- 2 cups / 480g sour cream
- ½ cup / 120g buttermilk
- 1 tablespoon / 20g kosher salt

Line a sheet tray with paper towels. Bring a large pot of heavily salted water to boil. Add the potatoes, turn the heat to low, and simmer them until close to tender, 10 to 12 minutes. Drain and then lay out the potatoes on the towel-lined sheet tray to cool. Do not refrigerate. Add the dill, chives, and parsley to a mixing bowl followed by the room temperature potatoes. Gently mix the herbs and potatoes. Next add the mayonnaise, sour cream, buttermilk, and salt. Fold in the liquid ingredients until all is well combined, then use the flat of a spoon to smash some of the potatoes.

Prepare the potato salad a day in advance, as the flavors marry and improve overnight.

7

SLOW SMOKE

A Return to Barbecue

As both a food and a culture, barbecue is bigger now than probably at any time since the invention of gas and electric cooking. Everywhere I look, a new barbecue place has popped up, and I love that so many people are stepping up to the challenge of slow-smoking meat.

It never gets old. Each new hunk of meat, each day's weather, each smoker, and each piece of firewood presents a different set of circumstances to be figured out by the cook to achieve the best results. So, in a way, barbecue is a perpetual puzzle that keeps you sharp and thinking, just like a sudoku or crossword. Despite its puzzles, cooking barbecue provides ample time for peaceful rumination when you sit by as the fire slowly breaks down a piece of wood into the smoke that will curl around the meat on its way out of the stack.

This chapter is a return to that restful moment. At its heart is a new and refined brisket recipe that reflects our ever-evolving methods of smoking at the restaurant. This is how we cook our briskets today—and it yields even better results than when we published *Franklin Barbecue* in 2015. Some of the changes are subtle, but over the course of twelve hours, even subtle differences become significant. And when I say *brisket recipe*, I really mean an almost stream-of-consciousness narrative, since so many of the details are related to feel and observation.

In addition to brisket, I've included recipes for smoking duck, turkey, baby back ribs, prime rib, and beef ribs. The techniques are all similar, so the skill you develop in managing your smoker will serve you well going forward. The recipes are geared for a Texas-style offset smoker. In fact, I tested all of these recipes on the new Franklin Pit described in chapter 2. But, of course, you could easily do them on a bigger, more professional pit, or, if you don't have any of this equipment, the techniques and visual cues will work on any other kind of smoker or on a PK grill, Big Green Egg, or kettle-style grill rigged for smoking.

Have fun with the process. Great backyard barbecue has always been a mixture of relaxation and application, a chance to commune with your food, your yard, and yourself. As wise people say, the path is the goal; though, with smoking meat, the goal is also the goal, so enjoy your delicious barbecue.

THE ULTIMATE BRISKET

The brisket recipe from *Franklin Barbecue* runs eleven pages, and—judging from the amount and intensity of feedback I've received over the years—it was really helpful to lots of folks. I truly don't have enough fingers to count the number of times someone has come up to me and said, "That brisket recipe changed my life!" I'm thrilled to have been able to help out, and people continue to ask me brisket questions often, even with the original, detailed recipe out there.

Every brisket that you smoke is a journey unto itself in which every step is filled with uncertainty, choice, and vagary—at least until you get comfortable with piloting this great big barge of meat. It's just one of those things where the investment of time and resources is so great that people are afraid of making mistakes and seek close guidance. That's hard to give when such elemental variables as wood, fire, smoke, and meat are involved, but here is, once again, my attempt to provide as much help in as much detail as possible—with the caveat that the best way to find answers to your questions is to cook a lot of briskets.

We never stop learning and growing— even at Franklin Barbecue. Over the years, I've evolved in my brisket thinking. Not that I've reinvented the beefy wheel or anything, but the technique we practice at the restaurant has shifted a bit and gotten tighter and more precise in certain ways. In fact, as the popularity of barbecue has grown around the country, brisket—which was traditionally a Texas thing—has become more widespread. Many people are looking at solutions for the inconvenient truth about brisket: that the length of time it takes to cook swallows up a day and pushes your levels of endurance and commitment. Today, approaches such as hot 'n' fast brisket, in which the meat is done in six hours as opposed to twelve hours, have become popular in barbecue circles. While I applaud anything that makes people happy, I don't think a brisket that I want to eat can be done in such a short time—at least not one with the qualities I consider to be important: sweetly smoky, peppery, and texturally rich bark; profoundly moist meat whose fat has rendered; a pliable texture that doesn't fall apart in the flat and melts in your mouth in the point; and even cooking throughout the meat.

Our brisket has always come out well, but over the years I've adjusted many of the specifications. I'll take you through them step by step. A number of these tweaks rely on good fire management, something we're all capable of doing if we practice and pay attention.

Basically, the idea with this revised brisket technique is instead of going hotter and quicker at the start, you want to ease into things. You don't have to go too low because a low temperature will make the cook go way too long, and you want to avoid a dirty fire at all costs. But you don't want to jump out of the gates at 275°F either.

The first problem you encounter with a hotter and faster technique—and I'm not even talking about the aforementioned hot 'n' fast approach that starts at 300°F—is that the brisket's edges dry out and moisture puddles up and concentrates in the middle, changing the cooking dynamic. The finesse in cooking a great brisket is in cooking the whole surface evenly because it inherently does not want to cook that way. If you look at a brisket, you'll see one part that's thin and lean and one part that's thick and fatty, and they don't cook at the same rate or have the same needs. The challenge is to accommodate this discrepancy in a way that allows all parts to come out beautifully.

PREPARING THE MEAT

Once you've completed your cooking lists, gather your tools, equipment, and ingredients.

- 1 whole (packer-cut) brisket
- Yellow mustard for slathering
- Coarse salt
- 16-mesh ground black pepper
- Apple cider vinegar for spritzing

Choosing Brisket

We cook around one hundred twenty Creekstone Farms prime-grade briskets every day at the restaurant. These are excellent pieces of meat and, when Creekstone is at its best, there are few operations that can compete. Theirs are well-tended Black Angus cattle that spend all but the last few months of their lives on grass before being finished on corn. I only buy briskets from cattle that have received no growth-promoting hormones. We pay a premium for these, but it's worth it without question—they

cook better, taste better, and are happier animals. The cattle are slaughtered humanely in a facility designed by legendary scientist and animal behaviorist Temple Grandin in a way that preserves the integrity of the animal, its meat, and the workers. The brisket is fabricated—cut from the larger side of beef—to precise specifications that Creekstone and I worked on together. When you're cooking as many briskets per day as we do, consistency is paramount.

If you're a home cook who cooks brisket only occasionally, consistency is less important, but you still want to start with a good-quality cut. Evaluate the meat carefully before you cook it and consider its various characteristics. Namely, how fatty is it (intramuscular, subcutaneous, and external)? I'm always looking for as much internal marbling as possible. How was it raised (is it a grass-fed cow from a local farmers' market, which means the meat is likely leaner and tougher with much less fat, or was it finished conventionally at a feedlot)? I prefer grain-finished beef as opposed to grass-fed and grass-finished beef, which can sometimes come out too lean and grassy tasting after a long cook. As always, I recommend that you cook a packer-cut brisket, which is a whole brisket that includes the full muscle—both the point and the flat (see Brisket Terminology, opposite). A brisket in the 12- to 14-pound range is ideal.

Trimming

My trimming method hasn't really changed, but I want to reiterate that trimming is a very important step. It sets you up for success or failure during what is going to be a long cook.

When preparing to trim a whole brisket, take a second to look past its bulky, clumsy form and imagine the sleek, aerodynamic shape that exists inside of it. You want to whittle a Ferrari out of a big, dumb hunk of flesh. Imagine the smoke in the cooker smoothly flowing over and around the

BRISKET TERMINOLOGY

For the record and to get terminology clear, the *point* of the brisket is the thick, fatty half with a raised ridge, and the *flat* is the flat half that thinly tapers off. Also, when I refer to *forward* or *back* in the smoker, toward the smokestack is forward and toward the firebox is back. To me, the smoker is like a locomotive and the air comes in the rear, hits the fire, and pushes forward to the stack. I may be the only person who thinks of it like this, but now you know.

meat—like a car in a wind tunnel in an automobile ad. That's what you want to create here. The rub and the natural moisture of the brisket help to attract smoke, while a well-trimmed, fluid shape promotes even cooking.

I use a thin, slightly curved boning knife to trim because I like the precision and dexterity it provides. I trim more off the brisket than a lot of people do. What I mean is that I'm not afraid to cut away some strips containing a little meat if that's what I need to do to get the right shape. Mostly what I trim is fat, but sometimes there's lean in there. Nothing goes to waste, however; all those scraps go straight to the grinder for sausage. At home, I collect the trimmings and simmer them with water on the stovetop to create beef stock. My exact instructions for trimming a brisket are detailed in *Franklin Barbecue*, so have a look there if you want more information.

Tempering

You don't want to put a cold piece of meat in a hot cooker because the heat dries out the meat before it's thoroughly cooked. Food safety is always a concern, so I'm not telling you to leave a 31°F brisket out on the counter until it comes to room temperature (which would take forever, by the way). But letting it sit on the countertop for a couple of hours helps the meat temper a little, and, with brisket, a little goes a long way during a lengthy cook. (To

be clear, it takes four hours for bacteria to begin to replicate after meat hits the temperature danger zone of 41° to 135°F, so I'm not suggesting conditions that will endanger you.)

Applying the Slather and Rub

Once you've got your brisket all nice and trimmed, it's time to get it ready for the cooker. This is a good time to apply a slather. A slather isn't mandatory, but it helps the rub adhere to the surface of the meat. You can use almost anything that wets the surface, from water to vinegar to hot sauce, but I like good ol' French's yellow mustard. Squeeze out just enough to coat the entire surface of the brisket. And while you might think such a strongly and distinctively flavored substance would affect the final flavor of the meat, amazingly, it does not. (Some old-timers swear by mayonnaise.) Perhaps it adds a little savory complexity, but whatever its impact is, you certainly won't recognize the flavor like you do on a ballpark hot dog.

Next, apply the rub. Alongside the requisite one-to-one ratio (by volume, not weight) of salt and pepper, use any flavors you want. The purpose of a rub is twofold. Salt and pepper are critical flavors for brisket. The salt allows you to taste the meat in all of its glory. The pepper basically fuses with the exterior layer of fat to form the bark, which in turn mellows the spiciness of the pepper and creates massive amounts of umami. The other function of a rub is to attract smoke, which it does thanks to its uneven surface. This is why we use coarsely ground pepper. But you can also add anything else you want—cayenne, garlic powder, paprika, or a seasoning mixture, like Lawry's Seasoned Salt. We try out different rubs at the restaurant from time to time. It's all good, so long as you also have plenty of salt and pepper

Firing Up the Smoker

At least 1 hour before you cook, get the offset cooker going. (If you're using a grill to smoke, it should take 15 to 20 minutes to warm up.) You want to have arrived at and held your desired temperature for a good 15 minutes before adding the meat. (This is also a good time to work out the needs of your particular fire, especially, for instance, if you're at an event using a weird smoker and unfamiliar wood.) You and your smoker want to find equilibrium relative to whatever climactic conditions you might be experiencing that day.

In this revised technique, I start off with a lower temperature than I did in the past, aiming for about 260°F to start. So bring your cooker up to 260°F and hold that temperature for at least 15 minutes before putting the meat on. Make sure you have a good coal bed and a clean fire. How can you tell? Take a whiff. If the fire smells good, the meat is probably going to taste good because we taste with our noses. It's always wise to lean into your temps. By that, I mean ease into new temperature levels rather than raising temps too fast, overshooting the mark, and having to scramble to bring them back down.

Also, make sure you put a full container of hot water inside the smoker, as it helps the brisket cook faster and more evenly. I add it when I build the fire.

MEAT'S ON: HOUR 0 TO HOURS 4 TO 5

It's time to put your brisket on the smoker. You want the point facing back toward the firebox, where the smoke is coming from, and the flat facing forward toward the smokestack. On our cookers, the sweet spot is close to the stack. This is where the heat is most even, the airflow most fluid, and where meats tend to cook the best. So we position our briskets as far away from the firebox as possible. If your brisket's flat is really thin, consider angling the cut with the flat closer to the door, where it will theoretically encounter slightly less heat and consequently cook more slowly. Your task now is to simply let the brisket hang out for a few hours. Keep the temperature even and maintain as clean a fire as possible. You can relax during this time, but never stop paying attention.

HOW TO FIT THREE BRISKETS ON A SMALLER SMOKER

If you're cooking on a Franklin Pit or a similarly small cooker and want to squeeze on a third whole brisket, here's what you can try. First, use smaller briskets from the left side of the cow, as their similar shape will allow them to fit together better. Place them at a diagonal and parallel to one another but not touching in the smoke chamber. Place a wedge-shaped piece of wood (hack one off a log) behind the briskets, positioning it with the thin end facing back toward the fire to deflect some of the heat that would otherwise hammer the rearmost brisket. But for the best results, stick to one or two briskets.

Maintaining Smoker Temps

If you're cooking on a Franklin Pit or another smaller-size cooker, you may find it maddeningly difficult to hold a certain temperature. There is no digital thermostat for you to just "set it and forget it." Don't get discouraged. Indeed, part of the magic of these surprisingly sensitive hunks of steel is the variation in temperature. While small cookers are more sensitive than big ones, this general oscillation of temperature also creates a wide range of compounds in the smoke, adding to the complexity of the brisket.

If you think of your goal as maintaining a temperature range that averages around 260°F, you'll be fine. Concentrate on burning a clean fire, which is determined by the color of the smoke coming out of the stack—mainly avoid anything gray and sooty—and keeping active flames in the firebox. After a while, you will start to get a sense of how much fuel you need in order to maintain certain temperatures. Also, you'll start to feel a rhythm that's like the percussive thud of a speedboat skipping across the waves. Each bump is the burst of heat you get from a new log. As that burst climaxes and begins to fade, add another little piece of wood to keep your boat rising back up again and again.

Cut and split your wood in small pieces (see page 60). If your pieces are too large, they may give your fire a big burst of energy that causes the temperature to spike too high. Smaller pieces allow for more precision, so, if needed, split your mini logs into

even smaller pieces. These might feel like matchsticks to you, but feeding the fire small amounts of wood more frequently helps you maintain the pace and manage those gentle, rhythmic ups and downs. (This is true for any meat you cook on a smoker, not just brisket.)

Don't even open the smoker door for a peek during the first 3 hours. Your brisket will just be hanging out, gathering smoke. Between Hours 3 and 4, take a look and get your trigger finger ready to spritz.

Putting on the Spritz

The main reason for spritzing is damage mitigation. That is, you're slowing the drying of the brisket's ends while letting the middle cook. The midsection holds a lot of moisture that is constantly being wicked up and out of the flesh to the surface, where it evaporates. But at this time in the cook, there's more moisture than will evaporate naturally, so it can puddle up. This results in splotchiness on the exterior, which not only looks bad but also inhibits proper bark formation. Spritz on the parts that need cooling down so they keep pace with the midsection.

I use apple cider vinegar to spritz, but you could just as easily use water, wine, or orange juice. Perhaps the vinegar adds a little bit of acidity, though you don't taste it in the outcome. I guess I use vinegar out of habit and convenience because it's already in a spray bottle to use with ribs.

When you spritz, you don't want to cover the whole brisket. The goal is to hit certain parts accurately, so set your spray bottle to a fairly tight stream that expands to a couple of inches in diameter about 2 feet from the nozzle. The point of this precision spraying is to spray the ends, which dry out the soonest, without wetting the interior. Dry spots often occur at the end of both the point and the flat, along the sides if they're starting to harden, and at the crest of the little ridge on top of the point. Just

keep these areas wet, creating the evaporation that cools them and slows down their cooking speed.

In this first part of the cook, you allow the brisket to gather smoke. You've prolonged the cook and evened out the surface dehydration through spritzing. It should all be going well. The surface is beginning to dry out as the bark starts to form. The color is changing, going from its original red and white to a deepening brown. The smoke smells sweet. I still think of the brisket as sort of hanging out at this point, but now it's time to really start cooking!

THE FIRST PUSH: HOURS 4 TO 5 TO HOURS 6 TO 7

In this phase, you will ramp up the temperature and gather momentum so that when the brisket hits the stall in Hours 8 to 9 and you eventually wrap, you'll be able to cruise right through. Much of the art of cooking brisket is knowing when to push into the higher register of the desired temperature range as you move up to the next temperature goal. You never want to suddenly jump to a new temperature; you want to ease into it smoothly by pushing.

In the period between Hours 4 and 6, it's time to ramp up the temperature. Add a little extra fuel to increase the size of your fire and create more heat, allowing the cooker to rise to 270° to 275°F. You're moving up in temperature range because smoke accumulation is becoming less important (the brisket got plenty of smoke in the first 3 hours). At this stage, rendering fat is critical, and that happens more efficiently at these higher temperatures. You are not just rendering the external fat that forms the bark, however. What you are really trying to do is melt the intramuscular fat in a measured but decisive way. This takes a long time.

The first push is the prelude to getting ready to wrap. You really want to nail that bark. The pellicle (surface) is starting to dry, and the color continues to darken. Pay attention to the pellicle as it dries; it will begin to look crunchy. Keep your spritz going every 30 to 45 minutes.

As the subcutaneous and internal seam fats start to render, push temperatures as high as you can without doing any damage. I'm talking 280° to 285°F. The sides of the brisket will start to sweat, and the ends will begin to pull up a little. The fat is beginning to melt and drip off the meat, but it's not going to render a ton because we're only pushing a little. Push but don't rush, and keep checking and spritzing every 30 to 45 minutes.

As you move deeper into the cook, make decisions by sight, smell, and observation. Although I offer a loose schedule here, there's no exact timeline, so your senses, not the clock, are your guide. Your goal is to wrap 8 to 9 hours after putting the meat on. So, say, by 6 hours in, you'll be pushing pretty strongly, in part because the brisket is going to hit the stall and you want to gather momentum so the expected stall doesn't become the unsurmountable stall. (I have witnessed this in the past. Briskets that refuse after many hours to get over the hump will, of course, eventually finish, but by then, you will likely have missed your window to serve the food, leaving everyone disappointed and hungry.)

If the thin side of the flat starts to curl up or if it appears like you could just snap it right off, your brisket is well on its way to being burnt. It takes experience to anticipate this, but using your senses to diagnose a problem is a big part of becoming an expert brisket cook.

Wrapping occurs during the stall, so you want to think to yourself, "I need to push these temps, because if I stay at this low temperature, I'm never going to break through the ceiling." Keep your fire revved and your coal bed strong.

THE STALL AND THE WRAP: HOURS 8 TO 9

By Hour 8, the brisket will look almost cooked on the outside, but it still has a fair way to go. You held steady at around 260°F for the first 5 hours or so and then pushed up to around 275°F. Moving into Hour 8, the internal temperature of the brisket is probably 160° to 175°F. As the brisket sweats and moisture begins to pool on top, pay attention to the condition of the bark. It's imperative to keep the bark in good shape. You want it to start to get dry but then bring it right back. As it dries out more and more, you'll notice that the effect of the spritzing lasts a shorter and shorter amount of time. As the spritzing starts to become less effective, you'll begin to get ready to wrap.

The stall occurs when the evaporation of the moisture being squeezed out cools the brisket faster than the fire can heat it. (It's the same dynamic by which our perspiration cools us on a hot day.)

TEMPERATURE CHANGES

While I offer a rough temperature guide here, we change our cooking temps at the restaurant all the time, and they can vary by as much as 15° to 20°F, depending on the day. This is based on outside temperature and the briskets themselves, which do change in composition throughout the year. Just pay attention to the visual cues that I've given and adjust accordingly. You'll find your way after doing it a few times.

When this excess moisture is finally exhausted—at 7 to 9 hours into the cook—the meat begins its climb in temperature again. That's why this stage is called "the stall" and not "the end" or "the failure."

Leading up to the wrap you want the temperature to be solidly up around 285°F. Because you will be in the cooker spritzing and must open the door to take out the brisket, the smoker's temperature should be able to withstand all the activity.

Only experience can really tell you when it's time to wrap, but you know the brisket has entered the stall when its internal temperature has been hovering in the 160° to 165°F range and the bark is starting to dry out quite a bit. This is a good thing. The strategy here is to allow the bark to get a little bit crunchier than you want it to be, then wrap. Once the brisket is wrapped, the bark will remoisten in the steam of the package and ultimately become perfect.

Ideally, you wrap at the beginning of the latter half of the stall, but you've got a little bit of wiggle room to hover in that area if you need better bark. I like to wrap on the later side. You can sort of ride the wave and let the brisket hang out at a higher temperature to form better bark and then wrap. Or if you're in the stall and your bark is not quite right, you can back off your fire a bit and hang out in the back end of the stall before pushing out. If the temperature starts to go up and you haven't wrapped, you've gone too far. But don't wrap too early either. It's better to wrap on the back side of the stall than on the front side so you get as much bark development as possible before wrapping.

STALL OR NOTHING

Prior to recent times, when, you know, we didn't have science, the stall was the biggest mystery in barbecue. People were avidly watching the internal temperatures of their briskets when the seemingly impossible happened. After hours and hours of being in a hot smoker with its internal temperature gradually rising, the brisket's temperature would suddenly stop going up. Instead, it would flatline or even gradually drop a small amount. Then, apparently defying the ironclad laws of thermodynamics, it would remain this way for hours. It was spooky and added to the allure of briskets.

Naturally, home cooks panicked as this phase persisted. And when people panic, they tend to take dramatic action. Some pulled their briskets off the smoker, and, while the internal temperature might technically be "done" at 160° to 165°F according to USDA standards, when it was cut into, the brisket was anything but ready—the meat still tough as rope. Others built a huge fire to push the brisket out of this torpor, only to have to deal with out-of-control heat when the stall finally broke.

For a long time, even if professional barbecue cooks couldn't explain the evaporative cooling effect that was happening, they knew how to deal with it. And eventually science shined its revealing light inside the dark and smoky cooker and revealed the stall to be an obvious, if counterintuitive, occurrence.

Wrapping serves a few functions: (1) it keeps the brisket from taking on more smoke; (2) it concentrates the heat and discourages evaporation, which aids in breaking through the stall; (3) it helps the brisket retain moisture and fat; and finally, (4) during the endgame, it makes the cooked brisket much easier to handle and keeps the meat tightly cocooned throughout its lengthy resting stage.

Aluminum foil is the most popular wrap. However, I deliberately use butcher paper and have done so pretty much since the beginning. In a lot of ways, Franklin Barbecue has become synonymous with this technique. You can probably surmise some of the differences achieved by each material. Foil seals up the brisket somewhat hermetically, allowing little to no exchange with the outside environment. This locks in moisture but also encourages the meat to steam, which often results in a texture more like pot roast or corned beef and not the supple yet sliceable texture we think is ideal for brisket. (That said, if you don't have much fat to spare in a leaner brisket, foil is the better option.) To me, butcher paper is the ideal median between unwrapped and foil-wrapped. I truly appreciate the rustic nature of an unwrapped brisket, but that old-school method definitely results in meat that's drier to completely dried out and a bark that's more of a crunchy crust. When folded appropriately, butcher paper keeps the brisket tightly swaddled and allows some moisture to exit while retaining enough to keep the meat wonderfully moist.

On a table or countertop near the smoker, lay out the pieces of butcher paper you'll use to wrap the brisket (more details of the wrap are illustrated in *Franklin Barbecue*). There are two crucial points in this step: (1) Use enough paper to fold back over the bottom. That is, you need more than one layer of paper—my process uses three layers—so the bottom doesn't collapse when the package becomes filled with liquid and fat. (2) Wrap very tightly.

Spritzing the paper helps prevent it from taking moisture from the brisket. Wet it with anything you want—water, vinegar, or, better yet, melted fat. (Eventually the whole package will become saturated with fat anyway.) And don't ever wrap on a really cold table, as it will suck some of that hard-earned heat out of the meat.

Use a towel that you don't mind getting dirty to fetch the brisket from the smoker and take it over to your wrapping paper. Fold it quickly yet gently. Make it as tight as you can, then return the package to the smoker.

ENDGAME: HOURS 9 TO 12

With the brisket tightly wrapped in butcher paper, you can really start to push the temperature. Aiming for 300° to 310°F is a great target, but tread lightly because you can do a lot of damage at this point if you push too hard. Confoundingly, you can also mess up a perfectly great cook if you don't push hard enough. (Heck, if you want, you could even take the brisket out of the smoker and finish it in the oven, as temperature is the only important variable at this point. Younger me was firmly against doing this for reasons of orthodoxy, but older me really values a good night's sleep. Let circumstances dictate your actions. If you're having a good time outside and enjoying your fire and company, why not just keep it going?)

From here, you will continue cooking in the temperature range of 300° to 310°F for 3 to 4 hours. How long precisely? This is where it gets tricky because you can't see the meat anymore. If you haven't cooked thousands of briskets, this can be a daunting decision. Even I get rusty sometimes, and the same goes for our cooks at the restaurant. If someone has been off for three days, it often takes a day to get back the proper feel.

You can and should use a digital thermometer to gauge the internal temperature, which will be 175° to 180°F coming out of the stall. That will put you in the range, but it can't be your only metric because, as we learned during the stall, temperature doesn't equal doneness when it comes to brisket. The endgame is a race to break down the brisket's tough, fibrous collagen into soft, delicious gelatin before all the fat has been rendered out.

You want to try to take the brisket off the cooker in 12 hours. So if you wrapped at 8 to 8½ hours, you have 2 to 3 hours left to achieve the desired texture. This is subjective and requires experience, but eventually you will get a feel for how the fibers are breaking down and the fat is rendering.

Give the brisket a gentle little prod by placing a towel around the package and picking it up with your thumbs on top and your fingertips underneath. Press lightly with your fingers. Is it starting to feel tender or is it still hard as a rock? If it's the latter, increase the temperature a bit because you may be cooking too slowly. If you've fallen behind schedule (and are the gambling type), you could push your temperature to 325°F, but I would never go past that. You should only raise your temperature that high if you have enough moisture and fat in the package to keep the brisket from drying out (which you might surmise if you wrapped really early, as it wouldn't have evaporated as much). If you've got the moisture, you can push really hard. If it's not there, lay off and keep your temperature around 300°F, and let it run its course. If the brisket feels tender with a few tougher spots, you still have a little way to go. Check frequently and you'll feel those areas of tautness begin to recede. If the brisket is extremely pliant, you are getting close.

The Pull

One thing to keep in mind during the brisket's endgame—and when planning the whole cook—is that resting the brisket is part of the cooking process and pulling it off the heat is only done when you have a plan for its carryover. The heat that the brisket has accumulated for all these hours will carry over and continue the cooking even after you've pulled it. This is not a minor, post-cook situation that you can pay attention to by choice. You have to think about it and plan for it, as the carryover affects your decision on when to pull the brisket.

What are the climactic conditions of the brisket's resting place? Is it a hot summer day or a cold winter evening? Are you in the sun or in the shade? You must consider questions like these when you look into the future and try to guess how your brisket is going to carry over. If you think it has a lot of momentum—say, if you finished really hot at 315° to 325°F—pull it early to compensate. If it's going to begin a rapid cooldown—if it's smaller or finished at a lower temperature—let it go farther down the path in the smoker.

At some point, the brisket must come off the heat. This is when you discover whether you set yourself up for success on the front end and had enough fat render in a well-insulated package that didn't dry out the edges too badly. Doneness typically begins to occur when the internal temperature of the brisket is in the low range of 200°F. In *Franklin Barbecue*, I suggested that 203°F was my magic number. Today, I'll take anything up to 208°F or even 210°F in concert with the textural feel of the brisket as described previously.

To take the temperature of the brisket, pinch the stem of a digital thermometer between your thumb and a finger 1 to 1¼ inches from the tip (to ensure you don't puncture the bottom). Insert the thermometer through the wrap at a perpendicular angle into the middle height of the center of the brisket, as this is the last part to get tender. Or go in through the side, halfway up, and be sure you don't let any liquid spill out.

To pull the brisket, pick it up and set it on a baking sheet. You might want to put a little towel over it if, say, you're outdoors and the day is chilly or windy and you want to slow down the cooling. Keep it wrapped; you never unwrap a brisket until just before you're ready to serve it.

Rest in Peace

There's an art and a process to holding a brisket. (I once spoke at Texas A&M for an hour and a half just on holding, which is almost as long as you might hold a brisket that you've just cooked!) Many people cook their brisket well before they serve it because you never know how long it's going to take and you should always include an hour or two of wiggle room.

Once you've pulled the brisket, plan to let it rest for up to 3 hours in a warmish, room temperature environment. This span will vary depending on when you want to eat. Do not rush your brisket into a cooler or ice chest, as many people advocate. Most coolers have insulation, which might encourage the internal temperature of the brisket to climb too high, especially if it is large and has a lot of momentum or if you're resting several briskets next to one another. And definitely don't put your brisket directly into a warming oven for the same reason.

Use your digital thermometer to measure the internal temperature occasionally and get a sense of the brisket's rate of cooling. Just as you gauged the carryover potential while deciding when to pull the

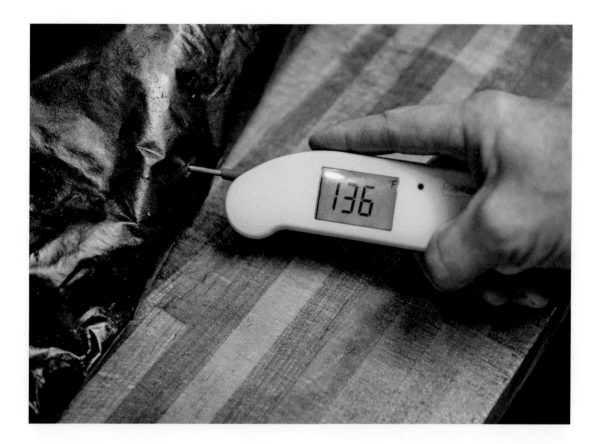

brisket, now you want to gauge where the internal temperature will settle down. The technique for checking temperature during rest is a little different from the method you used to determine the pull. Using the same hole in the butcher paper, test the middle of the brisket, then pull the thermometer out of the meat but not out of the package. Reinsert the thermometer and angle the probe to the left and then to the right to measure the temperature of both the flat and the point.

Monitor these temperatures. You are looking for something in the range of 140° to 150°F. If the temperature is descending really fast (go by instinct here, but it should descend quite gradually), you may want to put the brisket into a 140°F oven soon so it lands gradually, like an airplane. (Most ovens only go as low as 175°F, but you can finesse it by

turning the oven on and off, much like you managed the heat when adding wood to the smoker. Bread proofing boxes also work well.) But if it's slowly cruising along on its descent, you can probably let it be until it gets much closer to 140°F. You just have to get a feel for it. You want to let it mellow and cool. The fats are still rendering, the collagen is still converting, and the muscles are still pushing out moisture. Once the brisket peaks and the temperature starts to descend, it relaxes. It reabsorbs some moisture and settles down while the flavors continue to meld.

When the brisket is in the range of 140°F, you can open and serve it or, if you want to hold it longer, put it into a 140°F oven for up to 2 hours. At this point, the brisket won't get any better, so serve it as soon as you can.

CARVING AND SERVING

Carving your brisket at any temperature warmer than 150°F will result in you burning your hand and the brisket falling apart. The meat pulls itself together while cooling and is much more pleasant to eat when you can cut full slices. (Also, please do not hold up a chunk of meat and squeeze out the juices to impress your friends. That only ruins what you worked so hard to cook!)

In brief, my method of carving brisket evolved out of the imperative to always cut across the grain. The trouble with carving a brisket all in one direction is that the point and the flat have differently oriented grains. So first I cut the brisket in half across the middle, right where the flat and the point meet, which you can easily determine because the point starts to bulge at that spot.

- To slice the flat: First, cut off the pointy tip. It's mostly bark and might be crispy, but it's usually delicious and you can slice it in half into two little nibbles. Then, making ¼-inch-thick slices—each against the grain with the same amount of fat, meat, and bark—begin to fan out the slices so you arrive uniformly at the horizontal bias where you first split the brisket.

- To slice the point: First, cut the whole thing in half lengthwise. Cut the leaner, tighter section against the grain into even fanned slices ⅜-inch thick. The other side isn't as servable because of all the fat. You might get a couple of slices of meat off of it, but we don't serve the rest to guests. It's very, very fatty. You can save that meat to make into stock, add to the beans recipe in *Franklin Barbecue*, give to your dog, or whatever you want.

There are lots of details and photographs of my carving method in *Franklin Barbecue*, so check that out if you want to learn more. Enjoy!

BIG GREEN EGG BRISKET

Forgive me if I vent a little. Or am I gushing? I'm honestly not sure. The question of whether or not you can produce great brisket on a Big Green Egg (BGE) has been a preoccupation of mine for a very long time. And in many ways, this question is a microcosm of my relationship with the BGE in full: I respect the heck out of it—and I truly admire and appreciate the company and the people who work there. I relish the quality of a BGE's every detail, just as I respect the people who sing its praises and are so enthusiastic about using it. And yet, I don't quite know how to get the most out of it for the way that I like to cook.

Allow me to explain. Many people have told me that they do great smoked brisket on the BGE. I've always been a bit baffled by that claim because the smoking dynamic of the BGE is so different from the offset cooker that I deem essential for making classic Central Texas BBQ. Yes, the BGE is a powerhouse and a revelation when it comes to maintaining stable temperatures, which is indeed an important aspect of smoking brisket. But the nature of the BGE's main heat source (charcoal, not burning wood), the composition of its smoke (made of smoldering, not burning, wood), and the difference in airflow (not as violently convective as an offset) are so different that I wondered how it could be done.

Over the years, I have questioned and conversed on the topic of brisket with every BGE diehard that I've met. To a one, they maintain that not only can it be done but it turns out

great. I like people, and I trust (many of) them, so, while deep inside my bones I had my doubts, I also had faith in their virtue and have thus continued to exist in a state of belief that true Central Texas brisket can be done in a BGE.

Now, after many attempts and lots of pondering, I share with you my results. Also, let's remember that an attempt at brisket is not like attempting to grill a steak. We're talking a lot of hours here. It takes *work*. Cutting to the chase: Good brisket is indeed possible on the BGE, but it's not a Franklin brisket or even necessarily a classic Central Texas–style brisket. It's a BGE brisket, and that's not a bad thing. It has good flavor and a classic texture, but it doesn't taste or feel exactly the same as it does from an offset.

Following is the technique that I arrived at, which involves gentle modifications of the BGE to make it function more like a powerful smoker than a stable outdoor oven and grill. I won't go into as much detail as I did in The Ultimate Brisket (page 179) because there's a lot of crossover between the two. If you've got a BGE and want to try this, I suggest you read that recipe and sort of fuse the two in your mind. I've just presented the BGE highlights here.

THE MODS

For these modifications, I wanted to find simple solutions that could be accomplished easily and affordably with a visit to your local hardware store.

One thing that I have thought about for years and even suggested to a number of people but never tried myself is to attach a smokestack to the top of a BGE. This basic mod is meant to increase the draw of air through the egg and get fresher smoke pulling through as fast as possible. To do this, I bought and connected together two pieces of inexpensive galvanized-steel duct pipe, each six inches in diameter and two feet long, that I found in the HVAC section of my local hardware store. The top vent of my BGE was a bit smaller in diameter than the pipes, so I made a ring of crumpled aluminum foil and wrapped it around the interior of the pipe to get a tight fit. After the coals had started and were burning well, this makeshift stack helped the draw quite a bit. The only downside is that you have to take it off every time you open the lid. If I'd had more time and desire, I would have figured out how to attach it more permanently. But if you don't open the lid too often, it's not that inconvenient to just remove the stack and replace it after you've closed the lid.

My second mod was to use an angle grinder with a masonry blade to cut a crescent-shaped piece out of the smoke deflector plate—BGE calls it the convEGGtor plate—to give me a place to drop fresh wood chunks and/or hot wood coals into the egg. This is easier to do than it sounds and provided the access to the coals that I wanted. (In general, I think it's a handy modification—it doesn't change the internal dynamics very much and gives me a place to add wood and coals for longer smokes, no matter what I'm cooking. Shortly after I cut the plate, I cooked pizzas on the egg, and it was fine. Another solution is to buy two convEGGtor plates, one to modify and the other to leave as is.)

My final adaptation was to place three firebricks on top of the smoke deflector plate and then a half grate on top of the bricks. This was to get the brisket up a little higher in the cook chamber, where I hoped it would find more top heat to balance out the intensity of the heat from below, since the coals are located directly underneath the brisket. Also, hopefully the smoke would swirl and focus a little more before shooting up through the stack. Plus, the raised grate gave me a space to slide a drip pan under the meat.

With this setup, I burned charcoal and several post oak wood chunks in the bottom, as one would normally do to smoke something on the BGE. The only other casual technique that I employed was to prop the lid open slightly by sliding a pair of tongs in. Even with the lid slightly ajar, smoke did not escape through that opening, instead continuing strongly through the smokestack. The bit of extra air intake through the lid seemed to clean up the fire a fair bit and make for better-quality smoke.

It's important to measure the temperature of a BGE independently at grate level. The installed thermometer reads up at the top of the chamber, and I've often found it to be as much as 20° to 30°F higher than what I measure at grate level.

THE METHOD

With these mods in mind, you can, for the most part, follow The Ultimate Brisket recipe. All the basic temperatures and times will vary depending on the size and fat content of your brisket anyway.

Using charcoal and wood chunks, get the BGE fired up to 260°F (this is actually easier to do than in an offset). Put your brisket on at this temperature and let it ride for about 3 hours. You'll have to open the lid every 30 minutes or so to refresh the wood and coals. To have hot coals ready to put in, keep a chimney going next to the egg. When you take a few coals out

of the chimney, dump fresh ones into it to keep it going. Now is when a side fire would also be helpful. You could just keep adding fresh coals.

The BGE is good at conserving moisture. However, if you smell fat starting to burn, feel free to add water to the drip pan.

After 3 to 4 hours, push the temperature up to 275°F or so and begin spritzing any edges where you see the bark drying out.

After 6 hours, turn the brisket because the bottom side gets hotter than the top side from the smoke deflector plate being heated directly from the coals. Now bump the temperature into the range of 285° to 290°F.

After about 8 hours, when the internal temperature is in the 160° to 165°F range, you should be entering the stall, and it's time to think about wrapping in butcher paper. Wrap the brisket and return it to the smoker.

At this point, if the brisket has a good deal of fat, you can raise the temperature to around 300°F. But if you're not confident that you have a really well-marbled piece, keep the temp at 285°F to be on the safe side. You could even put the brisket in the oven now if you don't feel like managing the fire anymore. But it's very easy to maintain temperature in a BGE, so you might as well leave it in. You can also remove the stack because the process is just about baking from now on.

Follow the instructions in The Ultimate Brisket recipe to measure the temperature properly and pull the brisket from the heat when the internal temp is between 205° and 208°F. Let the brisket rest until it cools to the 140°F range before you slice and serve it.

BABY BACK RIBS

Many people associate Texas barbecue solely with beef, but there's a large pork culture here too. At the restaurant, we've always served pulled pork, and pork ribs are one of our most popular items. But those are spareribs, which are different from the ubiquitous baby back ribs. I detail our sparerib method in *Franklin Barbecue*, but baby backs require a somewhat different method.

First and most important, baby back ribs do not come from baby pigs . . . nor does "baby got back." They're called *baby* because they're smaller than spareribs, even though they come from the same part of the rib cage. Baby backs are cut from the rib bones at the top of the pig near the backbone, where the bones have more of an arc. Cut farther down the bone, spareribs are bigger, straighter, more marbled, and meatier, which is why we favor them at the restaurant.

Because of their popularity, baby backs tend to be a bit more expensive than spareribs. A rack of baby backs weighs in the range of two pounds, half of which is bone. The other, meaty half can often be demolished by one person in a single sitting, making them a nice and tidy order. People love baby backs for their toothsomeness—when they offer a little resistance to the front teeth. (But that chewiness also makes me wonder if they've had ones that are properly tender.)

In general, the meat of baby backs is leaner than sparerib meat, which affects how they are cooked. I advocate going a bit hotter and faster than with spareribs because of this leanness. You don't want to exhaust the fat that baby backs do have over a long cook.

It's quite common to wrap baby backs tightly in aluminum foil. However, I stumbled on a technique of partial wrapping, and I like it. You make a foil boat to steam the underside while drying out the meaty top. The opening in the foil allows some of the liquid to evaporate, but enough moisture is retained to achieve optimum tenderness. The boat also allows the top to get perfectly colored without the whole rack drying out. The goal is for the meat to be plenty tender without completely falling apart. In other words, it should be resistant enough that your teeth still have something to do.

Cook time: 4 to 5 hours
—
Serves 4

- Two 2-pound racks baby back ribs
- Kosher salt
- BBQ Spice Rub (page 112) or your favorite rub
- Apple cider vinegar for spritzing
- 1 cup Rye BBQ Sauce (page 122) or your favorite BBQ sauce, warmed

Lay the rib racks, membrane-side up, on a large baking sheet. Salt the membrane side and then add the rub. Flip the racks and spread the rub on the meat side. Lightly spritz the vinegar over the rub on the meat side. Let the racks sit while you get your fire going in the smoker.

Fill a pan with water and place it in the cooker. Bring the temperature to around 300°F to start. Place the racks, meat-side up and perpendicular to the door, in the cook chamber close to the smoke-stack. Spritz the racks frequently with the vinegar to keep the surface moist but not too wet.

After about 2 hours, the ribs should be taking on a nice, tawny mahogany color. Now it's time to prepare the aluminum-foil wrap. Tear off two pieces of heavy-duty foil each 16 inches long and lay them on a table. Pour about ¼ cup of the warm sauce onto each piece of foil, extending it along the center. Using tongs, transfer each rib rack to a piece of foil, placing it on top of the sauce. Bring up the sides of the foil and wrap them tightly around the edges of the ribs, leaving the crest of the meat (a strip about ½ inch wide down the center of the rack) exposed. Make sure the package is tightly secured.

Spritz the crest of the meat with vinegar and then coat with the remaining sauce, dividing it evenly. Return the racks to the cooker and raise the temperature to 310°F. Cook for up to 2 hours more, with the meat exposed and spritzing if needed, until the ribs start to feel done. To test, using a toothpick, poke the meat side between the bones; if the toothpick slides in and out with ease, the ribs are tender and done.

Pull the two rack boats from the cooker and let the racks rest, still in their boats, until cool enough to handle. Slice between the ribs and transfer to a platter. Drizzle with the beautiful sauce in the bottom of the foil boats. Serve immediately.

BEEF RIB

For some aficionados, the beef rib is the Texas barbecue pièce de résistance—yes, even over brisket—and I may be one of those people. In fact, the beef rib is probably the source of my favorite single bite in all of barbecue. From a rib that's been off the pit for just a little while and is still pretty darn hot, grab one of the top-front corners of the meat with your fingers and pull a little to loosen it. Continue to pull, twisting, and draw out the tender meat like a core sample. If you can slide out all the fibers of that little string in one piece, you have an excellent beef rib. It's so flippin' good!

On the whole, beef ribs are impressive and indulgent—big, solid, and on the bone. We use three-bone plate ribs cut from low on the rib cage, which provides a nice, thick bone that looks great. What exactly are the plate ribs? On a cow, part of the brisket muscle reaches underneath the rib cage and terminates between ribs five and six. For our beef ribs, we use the cuts from the next three ribs—six, seven, and eight. They're just the right size and come from the same animals that supply our briskets. If you can, get your plate ribs fresh, never frozen.

I like to do a slather on ribs because they're typically a lot drier than brisket once they are removed from their plastic wrapping (if that's how they came). I use a standard commercial hot sauce, such as Crystal Hot Sauce. You might think this flavor would be too intense, but, as with all slathers, by the time the rib is cooked,

there's so much fatty richness and smoke that you can't taste the slather. My hope is that the additional acidity helps the rib taste just a tad more balanced. Ribs are so dense and rich that they can take a lot of seasoning. For the rub, I use our BBQ Spice Rub (page 112) or Lawry's Seasoned Salt mixed with freshly ground black pepper and kosher salt. Tallow—which you can render yourself from beef fat, buy from a good butcher or online, or simply save from a brisket cook—forms the basis of the mop, as it protects and drenches the gorgeous rib meat at the same time.

Be aware that this is an incredibly rich dish, and most people can only eat a few bites before moving on to less unctuous fare. At least that's how it is for me, so I don't center a meal around a beef rib. Instead, I offer it as a delectable bite alongside other meats.

A beef rib is easy to cook, and I have a method that I like for optimal deliciousness. At the restaurant, we do beef ribs only on Saturday and Sunday, billing them a weekend special. Unlike brisket, beef ribs never get wrapped and take about eight hours in the smoker. This is not exactly how we do them at the restaurant because that process is a bit more elaborate, but it makes maybe the best bite of rib I've ever had, so enjoy.

Cook time: 8 hours
——
Serves 6

- One 4-pound three-bone beef plate rib
- Crystal Hot Sauce or your favorite hot sauce for slathering
- BBQ Spice Rub (page 112) or your favorite rub
- Apple cider vinegar for spritzing

Tallow Mop

- 1 cup / 200g tallow (rendered beef fat)
- 1 cup / 240g apple cider vinegar
- ½ yellow onion, chopped
- 16 garlic cloves, crushed
- Few dashes Crystal Hot Sauce or your favorite hot sauce
- 1 squirt yellow mustard

Slather the entire rib with hot sauce, then lay it, bone-membrane-side up, on a baking sheet or sheet of aluminum foil. Apply the rub to the membrane side and then flip the rib and sprinkle additional rub on the top and sides. Let the rib sit while you get your fire going in the smoker.

Fill a pan with hot water and place it in the cooker. Bring the temperature to around 300°F to start. We start out hot because the amount of fat and bone mass can take the extra heat. Place the rib, meat-side up, in the cook chamber and let it rip.

To make the mop: Meanwhile, in a small saucepan, combine the tallow, vinegar, onion, garlic, hot sauce, and mustard; stir to mix; and keep warm in the smoker.

After 1 to 1½ hours, take a look. (I tend to check on beef ribs during the cook more often than I do brisket because I'm not worried about opening the smoker door too much and losing heat. It's already hot in there, plus the bone mass retains a lot of heat, protecting the meat.) Once you see any of the corners starting to dry out, begin to spritz frequently with vinegar. This needs to be done often to cool off the edges while waiting for the middle part to get hot. A beef rib will quickly get very crusty at this temperature, which is good, but you always want

to spray it down. So you're constantly letting it get crusty and then spritzing it down; letting it go too far and then bringing it back. Keep the rib pretty wet on the edges.

About 4 hours in (roughly halfway through the 8-hour cooking time), when the exterior starts to dry out a bit, transition from spraying with vinegar to mopping with the mop. Whereas before you let the bark get crusty and then you wet it down to prolong the cook, now you want to coat the exterior with fat, which protects and strengthens the crust you've just built. This is especially important because you're not going to wrap the ribs, so you need to take extra care to ensure the bark has a rich, thick, crusty texture.

Mop the rib with the mop all across the top. Never touch the surface of the beef rib with the actual mop head. Just let the liquid drizzle down on top of and over the ribs. Do this every 30 minutes.

There's no temperature to tell you when the rib is done. It will have reached a "done" temperature in the range of 205° to 207°F, but you're looking for tenderness, and that assessment is accomplished by feel. Using the spike of a Thermapen or other digital thermometer, poke gently in a few places to gauge tenderness. You are looking for general softness, but there's one specific test that will tell you exactly when you've nailed it.

There are two membranes surrounding the bones on a beef rib. The obvious one covers the underside of the bone. Many people remove it before cooking, but I don't. There's another membrane above the bones and just between the finger meat (that runs between the bones) and the fatty meat (above the bones). This is the thin membrane that's important. At spots just between the bones, probe down through the top very gently with your spike and feel carefully for that second membrane. When it yields with only a tiny bit of resistance, the rib is done. Be careful not to poke all the way through to the bottom, which can

cause a lot of moisture and fat to leak out. Because there's so much marbling on beef ribs, you have a very generous window here. It's hard to take a beef rib too far. Just don't miss that window because there's nothing sadder than a tough beef rib, which could happen if you don't cook it long or hot enough. You have to get a feel for it, but with practice, you'll get the hang of it.

When the rib is tender, transfer it to a baking sheet and let it rest until the internal temperature has lowered to 140°F.

Slice between the bones and serve immediately.

PRIME RIB

The process of cooking a prime rib in a smoker lies somewhere between cooking a beef rib (see page 203) and a côte de boeuf (see page 139). After all, the famed standing rib roast is just a larger bone-in hunk from which rib-eye steaks are cut.

To cook prime rib, salt it with kosher salt a day or two in advance and let it sit uncovered in the refrigerator. Get your smoker up to 250° to 275°F and put the roast in the cook chamber straight out of the fridge. Then let the temperature drop to around 225°F.

Let the roast cook, turning it occasionally, until you hit the desired internal temperature, about 120°F. This usually takes about 45 minutes per 1 pound of meat. As the roast starts to near that temperature, let the smoker temperature dip toward 200°F or even lower, until things line up. This inhibits massive carryover. Pull the roast at the temperature you desire, tent it with aluminum foil, and let it rest for only a few minutes to get that medium-rare texture, about 125°F.

With a very sharp knife, carve by first removing the bones in one neat slice (you can separate them later and give them to the bone lovers). Then simply slice the beef slab against the grain, perpendicular to the orientation of the bones, preserving the two end cuts for people who like more crust or slightly more done meat. Serve immediately with Horseradish Cream Sauce (page 140).

SMOKED DUCK

Even those who profess not to like duck will ravenously tear a smoked one apart after getting a taste of its crispy-crunchy, salty-sweet skin. Smoked duck is one of the most reliably delicious foods on Earth. This is a very straightforward preparation, and the smoking regimen is really easy. Using an offset cooker yields the best results and allows you to finish off the duck in direct heat in the firebox for extra-crispy skin. I've also had good success smoking duck on both the PK grill and the Big Green Egg.

There are several breeds of duck in the marketplace. The most common and popular is Pekin (aka Long Island duck), a white-feathered breed descended from the mallard. The Pekin has a mild flavor and decent fleshiness. Another common breed, the Muscovy, has more meat and a slightly more intense flavor and is also less fatty than the Pekin. If you cross a Muscovy male with a Pekin female, you get a moulard, which has more fat than the Muscovy and a nice broad breast. If you have trouble finding duck locally, you can order any of these from New York–based D'Artagnan (dartagnan.com). If you find a packaged duck at your grocery store, check its label to see if it has been brined. It is best if it hasn't been brined, but if it has, do not salt ahead of time.

There are only a few preparatory steps that help duck cook exceptionally well. The first is dry brining and prolonged air-drying. Duck has a lot of fat that renders out slowly, so having the skin as dry as possible helps.

I recommend that you air-dry in a refrigerator for at least two days, but I have gone as long as four days with no problem.

Basting, mopping, or spritzing adds a lot of beautiful flavor. I use a solution of maple syrup, red wine vinegar, and soy sauce, with a little garlic, orange peel, thyme, and black peppercorns for zest.

And finally, let the duck temper at room temperature before cooking.

Cook time: 4 to 6 hours
—
Serves 4

- One 4- to 5-pound duck
- Kosher salt

The Mop
- 1 cup / 340g maple syrup
- ½ cup / 120g vinegar of your choice
- ¼ cup / 65g soy sauce
- 4 garlic cloves, crushed
- 6 black peppercorns
- 8 thyme sprigs
- 1 orange

- Grapeseed oil or rendered duck fat for coating
- Freshly ground black pepper

Trim any extra fat from around the neck and inside the body of the duck. Leave about 1 inch of neck skin. (You can render down the trim and use it to coat the duck before cooking if you like.) Using a needle, the tip of a knife, or the sharp tip of a Thermapen, gently prick the skin all over, taking care not to puncture the meat. Try to angle the needle horizontally to the skin.

Weigh the duck and then calculate 1.75 percent of that total. Measure that amount in kosher salt (it's 25 to 30g, or just over 1 teaspoon, of salt per 1 pound of meat). Sprinkle the salt all over the skin of the duck.

Place the duck on a drying rack on a baking sheet and refrigerate for at least 1 day, preferably 2 days, or up to 4 days. Flip the duck once a day to dry all sides.

Before cooking, remove the duck from the refrigerator and let it temper at room temperature for no more than 2 hours. It's important to start with a duck that's not cold.

To make the mop: Meanwhile, in a small saucepan, combine the maple syrup, vinegar, soy sauce, garlic, peppercorns, and thyme. Quarter the orange and squeeze in its juice. Remove the peel, add to the pan, and discard the spent flesh. Place the pan over medium-high heat and bring the mixture to a boil, stirring occasionally. Adjust the heat to maintain a gentle boil and cook until reduced by about one-third, about 15 minutes. Remove the pan from the heat and allow the mop to cool. Strain it through a fine-mesh strainer into a bowl and set aside.

Preheat the smoker to 250° to 275°F. Gently coat the skin of the duck with grapeseed oil and then lightly coat all over with pepper.

Place the duck, with its legs facing toward the fire, in the cook chamber. Smoke for 4 to 6 hours, mopping every 30 to 45 minutes, without brushing the skin and dislodging the pepper rub. Duck can be cooked to a range of doneness, but look for about 185°F in the thighs and legs and 165° to 175°F in the breast for this one. Shortening the smoking time and removing it at lower temperatures tends to result in very tough meat in the legs.

When the duck is done, remove it from the smoker and let rest for 15 to 30 minutes. Then, if desired, crisp up the skin before serving by using tongs or a spear to hold the duck in the firebox over the coals, gently turning it. The skin will eventually blister, so remove the duck before it burns. If you are not using an offset smoker, place the bird over the coals on a grill or in the broiler of an oven (but be careful here, as the skin will blister very, very quickly—in seconds).

Using a carving or chef's knife sharp enough that it won't ruin the skin, remove the legs and thighs, then gently slice the whole breast off the bone and cut into angled slices. Serve immediately.

THANKSGIVING TURKEY

A couple of years ago, Stacy, Vivian, and I were visiting family for Thanksgiving, and I was tasked with cooking the turkey without a smoker. Faced with only an oven, I couldn't remember how to cook a turkey and had to search online videos for basic instructions! Of course, it came out just fine, but cooking a turkey in a smoker is clearly my second nature. I have smoked many, many Thanksgiving turkeys over the years, and they have all turned out delicious with this technique.

The key to this turkey is getting it well browned and then nailing the wrap. Unlike a brisket, which gets wrapped in butcher paper, the turkey is tightly wrapped in aluminum foil with lots of butter, which both enriches it and keeps the naturally lean bird from drying out. Because butter scorches and becomes unpleasantly dark and burnt tasting at high temperatures, I use an oil-butter blend, but you could also use ghee, or clarified butter. Because its milk solids are removed during the clarifying process, ghee has a much higher smoke point.

There are many options for buying turkeys these days, from the surprisingly affordable frozen specials at the grocery store to the shockingly expensive heritage birds that can cost well over a hundred bucks. I've had experience with both. Heritage breeds are an interesting proposition. As with heritage chickens, heritage turkeys are historic breeds developed over the last couple hundred years to promote various qualities: growth rate, life span, egg laying, and so on.

Today's commercial turkeys were bred to have more meat and to efficiently convert feed to that meat, though those traits have come at the cost of other qualities that make turkeys what they are, mating ability and egg fertility among them. Heritage turkeys have much more flavorful meat but less of it. That meat tends to be darker and tougher as well. And the birds are usually leaner. But if you like turkey with a deep, rich, more natural flavor, heritage is a good way to go. And the bones and carcass make incredible stock.

Although if you're looking to feed a large gathering, a well-grown commercial turkey is probably a better solution. They are not only less expensive and provide more meat but are easy to buy at most grocery stores. Their flavor, however, won't be as compelling as that of a heritage option.

This recipe is geared for a high-quality commercial bird. But, certainly, look for the best all-natural, unbrined turkey you can find. So many turkeys are brined these days, and I don't want to pay for added water.

- Unbrined turkey (whatever size you need, plan on between 20 and 30 minutes cook time per pound of turkey)
- Kosher salt
- Grapeseed oil for coating
- Freshly ground black pepper
- 1 pound / 450g oil-butter blend (such as SunGlow) or ghee (clarified butter), at cool room temperature

Weigh the turkey and then calculate 1.75 percent of that total. Measure that amount in kosher salt (it's about 8 to 10 grams, or just over 1 teaspoon, of salt per 1 pound of meat). Then sprinkle the salt evenly all over the skin of the turkey and in the cavity.

Place the turkey on a drying rack on a baking sheet and refrigerate for at least 1 day or up to 3 days.

Before cooking, remove the turkey from the refrigerator and let it temper at room temperature for up to 2 hours. It will cook much faster if not too cold.

Fill a pan with hot water and place it in the smoker. Preheat the smoker to 275°F. Gently coat the skin of the turkey with oil and then generously sprinkle with pepper. Place the turkey on the smoker's sweet spot—with mine, it's at the far end of the cook chamber, close to the smokestack—with the legs and body cavity facing toward the fire. (The dark meat of the legs and thighs can more easily handle the convective heat that courses through the smoker.)

Smoke the turkey until the skin has turned a deep golden brown, 2 to 3 hours—this is irrespective of weight, you're cooking for exterior doneness here, not specifically internal temperature. The goal is to get this deep brown shade by the time the internal temperature of the thickest part of the breast reaches about 130°F. Once the turkey has taken on all the color you want it to have, it's time to wrap with the oil-butter blend or clarified butter.

Lay out two large overlapped pieces of aluminum foil, shiny-side up, with a third long piece spread across them perpendicularly (see photos). Using a towel, gently lift the turkey out of the smoker without spilling any of the juices that have collected in the cavity and set it on the foil. Smear the oil-butter blend all over the exterior and inside the cavity of the turkey. You really want to pat it down, like you're a TSA agent. Now dust it with the pepper.

Now carefully flip the turkey breast-side down. Of course, it doesn't want to balance on the breast, so you'll have to rock it back and forth while gently bunching up the foil around it to create a little bunched-up nest that allows it to stand on its breast and retain all of its liquid. If you have

a temperature probe with a wire, insert it into the thickest part of the breast and keep the wire within the wrap so it comes out the top. Otherwise, a probe such as a MEATER can be inserted poking upward. Wrap the whole bundle fully and as tightly as possible so the oil-butter blend is always in contact with the meat.

Place the whole package in a large foil baking pan; this way, if the foil wrapping tears, you won't lose all that buttery liquid. When you place the turkey in its pan back in the cooker, keep it oriented with the thighs facing the fire. Bump up the temperature to somewhere in the range of 300° to 325°F. Cook the turkey until the breast is at about 153°F and the thighs register between 175° and 180°F, anywhere from 1 to 2 hours, or until done. The thighs should be a lot hotter than the breast. You really don't want to unwrap the turkey, but if you need to unwrap it to get a good temperature reading, do it carefully so you don't get burned. Then, if necessary, carefully rewrap and put the turkey back into the cook chamber until it has finished

cooking. (Don't let the buttery liquid pour out and travel down your pant leg and into your shoe, as I once did. Damn that hurt!) When the turkey has reached temperature, remove it from the smoker and let rest, fully wrapped, for 40 minutes to 1 hour.

Preheat the oven to 400°F or stoke up the heat in your offset smoker to that temperature. Unwrap the turkey and place it, breast-side up, on a baking sheet. Baste it with the buttery drippings, then slip into the oven or smoker for a few minutes to sizzle up the skin.

Transfer the turkey to a platter and carve. You'll have plenty of buttery liquid mixed with turkey juices pooled up at the bottom of the pan. Strain this and keep it warm; it's great stuff to spoon over the turkey.

Acknowledgments

Many people contributed—sometimes unwittingly!—to the making of this book, which was in many ways the most difficult of the three we've written. Some of this can be chalked up to the general weirdness inflicted by the pandemic, some to timing—we ended up building a lot of fires and doing lots of cooking in very hot weather—and some to life, as we and our families both experienced moves during work on this book. In the end, though, it was a great experience that we thoroughly enjoyed.

The first person we must thank is Wyatt McSpadden, yes, for his transcendent photography, but also for his sparkling personality and overall Wyatt-tude. Equal parts curmudgeon and comedian, he's simply a joy to be around, and his very presence while we're cooking and setting up a shoot gives us the confidence that it's all going to be okay. Throw in the hilariousness of his buddy act with his able and knowledgeable assistant Will Phillips, and we were always laughing even during the strenuous moments. Thanks, Wyatt and Will (and Nancy too!).

Of great help during some of those moments was Ha Lam, an experienced photographer and editor herself. What a boon to have her assisting on several shoots. Of course, David Hale Smith—skier, fisher, literary agent—thanks for building the foundation of all this, with a hat tip to all the other folks at Inkwell.

We also want to offer deep and sincere gratitude to the good folks at Ten Speed Press, who are truly responsible for this book. Namely, Julie Bennett, our editor who did an amazing job on the text while also bringing the project to life and remaining calming and patient throughout. What a pleasure it was to get to work (for the third time!) with designer Betsy Stromberg, who understands these books better than we do. Thanks so much to copyeditor Sharon Silva for literally thinking of everything, and to Doug Ogan, for offering some very useful edits. Thanks to Kathy Brock, proofreader extraordinaire, who worked magic down to the last comma. And to the amazing associate editor Ashley Pierce, who was always there: abiding and guiding, editing, and holding it all together. And thanks to Allison Renzulli, Joey Lozada, and Kristin Casemore for getting the word out, as ever.

Several people and their companies supported us in various ways with product. Notably, Alfonso Terrazas from Creekstone, a company that continues to support us generously with some of the best product in the world. Likewise, Aaron wants to acknowledge Anthony Charles, who has helped out often and on short notice, when we really needed to find certain items. And Jake and Chip from Made In were more than generous in supplying us with whatever sort of kitchen equipment we might have needed or even just wanted to try.

In Austin, Aaron offers a sincere declaration of gratitude to the whole staff at Franklin Barbecue, who not only helped out in numerous ways on many occasions, but are just awesome in general and manage to maintain good attitudes even when it's 105 degrees out. Likewise the entire office staff supplied endless and thorough support. Matt Gase and Jared Harmeier do way more than just make the Franklin Pit business go; they helped out a ton on this book in little ways that are greatly appreciated.

We thank Terry and David from the Little Longhorn Saloon on Burnet Road for the morning beers, when we got a couple of photos and had a pleasantly relaxed moment after some long days of shooting.

Vivian Franklin, what can we say? She made a great assistant and was full of creativity and energy and never hesitated to get involved. The ever vigilant Honey Franklin didn't set too many Honey traps in the backyard, starting in 2022.

Stacy Franklin—there no words. People tend to give Aaron credit for everything, missing the fact that almost nothing in the extended Franklin multiverse would happen without her industriousness, guile, intelligence, good sense, hard work, and heart. Jordan agrees, but also notes the importance of her wickedly sharp sense of humor, easy laughter, and intuitive sense of when it's time to stop fretting, sit back, and have a glass of wine.

With deep gratitude, Jordan wants to thank the Franklins for making him feel like family, as he lived in the Airstream in their backyard for weeks on end during production of this book. He felt like a welcome hobo every morning as he stumbled out of the trees and into their kitchen, poured himself the excellent coffee Aaron made (shout-out Travis Kizer of Barrett's Coffee), and chatted with them as they began their day.

Finally, Jordan, as ever, thanks his wonderful wife, Christie, for allowing him to own five grills that clutter the garage and also letting him make frequent trips to Austin to dwell in a backyard. A quick wink as well to Stanley Fallot MacDuf, whose relentless desire to walk and play usefully pried Jordan away from his well-worn laptop several times a day.

Index

V

vegetables
    coal-roasted, 167–68
    Pickled Vegetables, 120
    See also individual vegetables
vinegars, 96

W

wood
    chips, 58
    choosing, 57, 59
    chunks, store-bought, 66
    hard- vs. soft-, 54–55
    importance of, 53
    log size, 60, 63
    moisture content of, 58–59
    quality of, 53–54
    seasoned vs. green, 57–60
    tools, 63–64, 66
work gloves, 63

Typefaces: Hoefler & Co.'s Sentinel and Klim Type Foundry's National

Library of Congress Cataloging-in-Publication Data

Names: Franklin, Aaron, author. | Mackay, Jordan, author. | McSpadden,
  Wyatt, photographer.
Title: Franklin smoke : wood, fire, food / Aaron Franklin and Jordan Mackay
  ; photography by Wyatt McSpadden.
Description: California : Ten Speed Press, [2023] | Includes index. |
  Summary: "The ultimate guide to live-fire cooking and smoking at home,
  with recipes that will have you grilling up meat, vegetables, fish, and
  more like a Texas pitmaster-from the James Beard Award-winning team
  behind the New York Times bestseller Franklin Barbecue"— Provided by
  publisher.
Identifiers: LCCN 2022034856 (print) | LCCN 2022034857 (ebook) | ISBN
  9781984860484 (hardcover) | ISBN 9781984860491 (ebook)
Subjects: LCSH: Smoking (Cooking)—Technique. | Barbecuing. | Outdoor
  cooking. | LCGFT: Cookbooks.
Classification: LCC TX609 .F725 2023 (print) | LCC TX609 (ebook) | DDC
  641.6/165—dc23/eng/20220803
LC record available at https://lccn.loc.gov/2022034856
LC ebook record available at https://lccn.loc.gov/2022034857

Hardcover ISBN: 978-1-9848-6048-4
eBook ISBN: 978-1-9848-6049-1

Printed in China

Editor: Julie Bennett | Production editor: Ashley Pierce
Designer: Betsy Stromberg | Production designers: Mari Gill and Faith Hague
Production manager: Serena Sigona | Prepress color manager: Jane Chinn
Copyeditor: Sharon Silva | Proofreader: Kathy Brock | Indexer: Ken DellaPenta
Publicist: Kristin Casemore | Marketers: Joey Lozada and Allison Renzulli

10 9 8 7 6 5 4 3 2 1

First Edition